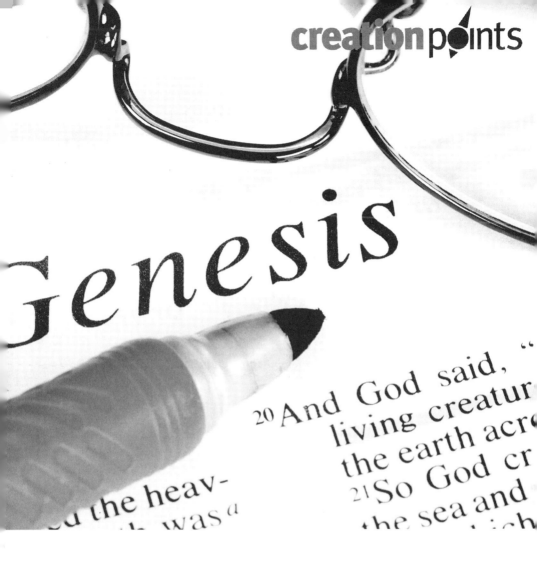

creation p◆ints

Genesis 1-11
A Verse-by-Verse Commentary

D1585885

Andy McIntosh

DayOne

Endorsements

Perhaps the most concise, clear and credible explanation of the first eleven chapters of the foundational book of the Christian faith. Andy McIntosh expertly shows how the text should be understood and the serious results if it is incorrectly interpreted. In addition, he applies the narrative to our day and the gospel. A significant and valuable study against the Christian scepticism of many commentators today.

Brian Edwards, author, lecturer and former pastor

In this profoundly helpful commentary on the opening chapters of the Bible, Professor McIntosh allows the Scriptures to interrogate the prevailing sophistry of our age. He writes simply under the banner of the perspicuity of Scripture as he engages with other commentators irenically but firmly. With his own formidable scientific knowledge he exposes the evolutionary pseudo-science which plagues our children's classrooms. Above all, he shows how these eleven chapters shine the spotlight on the coming Christ and how undermining their objective truth shatters the foundations of all Christian doctrine.

For the strengthening of your faith, examine Genesis 1–11 with Andy McIntosh!

Irving Steggles, pastor of Birchleigh Baptist Church, Kempton Park, Johannesburg, South Africa

It is refreshing to read a commentary on Genesis 1–11 that defends the chapters as literal history because that is clearly how God intended the chapters to be read. Professor McIntosh shows how the New Testament fully supports a literal interpretation of Genesis 1–11. The commentary will help Christians to have a better appreciation of God's work in creation and redemption.

Professor Stuart Burgess BSc (Eng), PhD, CEng, FIMechE, creation speaker and writer

It is a sure sign of the current crisis in Western Christianity that it has become exceptional, rather than normal, for Christian scientists of repute to be creationists—that is, to believe in the reliability and inerrancy of Genesis 1–11 without crossing their fingers behind their back! It is therefore very encouraging that Prof. Andy McIntosh is such a scientist and such a Christian. Here is a thoroughly helpful and accessible guide to Genesis 1–11 which brings into clear focus both the teaching of this passage and its scientific implications.

Roger Fay, pastor of Zion Evangelical Baptist Church, Ripon, and editor of Evangelical Times

Andy McIntosh brings together his expertise in science and the study of Holy Scripture in this readable and thought-provoking commentary. Christians discouraged by attacks on the biblical doctrine of creation will find this book to be informative, helpful, and more than a few breaths of fresh air.

Dr Joel R. Beeke, President, Puritan Reformed Theological Seminary, Grand Rapids, Michigan, USA

ISBN 978-1-84625-511-3

Unless otherwise indicated, Scripture quotations are from the **New King James Version (NKJV)**®. Copyright © 1982 by Thomas Nelson, Inc. Used by permission. All rights reserved.

British Library Cataloguing in Publication Data available

Published by Day One Publications
Ryelands Road, Leominster, HR6 8NZ
Telephone 01568 613 740 FAX 01568 611 473
email—sales@dayone.co.uk
web site—www.dayone.co.uk

Cover design by Rob Jones, Elk Design
Printed by TJ International

To the memory of
Roy Pibworth 1925–2004
(Wilstead Evangelical Church, Bedford),
who more than anyone schooled and mentored me
in biblical understanding.

Contents

About the author

ndy McIntosh DSc, FIMA, CMath, FEI, CEng, FInstP, MIGEM, FRAeS was until 2014 Professor of Thermodynamics and Combustion Theory at the University of Leeds. He has had a long scientific research career concerning mathematics, combustion and aeronautics, both in academia and in government establishments, and is now a visiting research professor at Leeds. He is married with three children living and one who died in infancy, and currently has six grandchildren. In the latter years of his academic work his research led him into the life sciences, with the study of the bombardier beetle, and the whole field of biomimetics—learning engineering solutions from nature. This research, inspired by the intricate design features of the beetle, has led to a novel spray technology being applied to fuel injectors, pharmaceutical sprays, aerosols and fire extinguishers. This research was awarded the 2010 Times Higher Educational Award for the Outstanding Contribution to Innovation and Technology.

He is the author of *Genesis For Today* (Day One, 5th edn. 2014), and has contributed to the books *In Six Days* (Master Books, 2009), *Should Christians Embrace Evolution?* (IVP, 2009), *The Delusion of Evolution* (New Life, 2010) and *Origins: Examining the Evidence* (Truth in Science, 2011). He has also contributed to TV and radio programmes to present the scientific evidence for creation and design, in particular *Newsnight* with Jeremy Paxman (BBC, 2006), *Sunday Sequence* with William Crawley (BBC Northern Ireland, 2006) and *The Big Questions* with Nicky Campbell (BBC, 2011). He speaks regularly both in the UK and further afield in connection with the importance of origins and against the reigning paradigm of evolution. He is listed at the Ratio Christi website for Student Apologetics (www.ratiochristi.org) and is a Logos Research Associate (www.logosresearchassociates.org). He is an associate speaker with Answers in Genesis (www.answersingenesis.org/bios/andy-mcintosh/) and has his own website, www.andymcintosh.org.

The book of Genesis is fundamental, opening God's revelation to man. Many Christians have tried to downplay the significance of Genesis by suggesting that the opening chapters of the book need not be taken in a plain, straightforward way. These people claim to be evangelical and yet argue for a non-obvious reading of the text. Typical of this viewpoint is John Walton's *The Lost World of Genesis One* (IVP Academic, 2009), in which the author, although accepting that the six days of creation were real days, then goes on to argue that the word 'create' (Heb. *bara*) refers to assigning functions rather than to a material creation, and that Genesis 1:1 is a literary introduction to the entire account, rather than a description of an initial creation event. Others, such as C. John Collins in his book *Science and Faith: Friends or Foes?* (Crossway, 2003), argue that the days are not to be taken as normal days and leave the door wide open for a theistic evolutionary perspective, while still claiming to be Reformed. Still others, such as John Lennox in his book *Seven Days That Divide the World* (Zondervan, 2011), argue for a series of days separated by possible gaps of long periods of time to accommodate evolutionary steps. This is similar to the progressive creation view advocated by Hugh Ross in *Creation and Time* (Navpress, 1994), who argues for an old earth and universe, with the days of Genesis 1 as long periods of time, along with a local Flood. Neither of these last two authors takes the obvious implication of Exodus 20:11 that, if the day of rest is twenty-four hours, then all the other six days are ordinary days as well, with an ordinary week. That is the whole point of the Sabbath command. The other point rarely addressed by authors of this camp (nor by those within the theistic evolution camp) is the fact that the Lord expressly says seven times in Genesis 1 that the creation was good and He underlines its perfection by stating that all that He had made was *very* good (Gen. 1:31). A six-ordinary-consecutive-day creation with no death is thus clearly taught in Genesis 1.

The full-blown theistic evolutionary view has been presented in such books as *Creation or Evolution: Do We Have to Choose?* by Denis Alexander (rev. edn. Monarch, 2014), and he in the UK and Francis Collins in the US typify a commonly held perspective which suggests that Adam need not necessarily have been created from dust, and that there could have been a whole raft of pre-Adamic hominids, with the Lord eventually taking one of them and breathing into him the breath of life. Alexander even allows for the possibility that some among the present human race may not be actual descendants of that particular person whom God appointed to be the head of the human race (he leaves open the possibility that some of the Aboriginals of Australia are not physically descended from Adam[1]). Many of these theological and scientific issues have been well answered in books such as my *Genesis For Today* (5th edn., Day One, 2014) and Norman Nevin (ed.), *Should Christians Embrace Evolution?* (IVP, 2009), the latter being a series of essays by experts in both the theology and the science of the origins debate. The major theological issue that the theistic evolution position encounters is that Romans 5:12–20 and 1 Corinthians 15:22–24 clearly teach that physical death came after the Fall and not before it. No serious student of the New Testament teaching on redemption can escape the conclusion that the physical death of Christ on the cross was necessitated because the penalty for sin was physical (as well as spiritual) death. Indeed, the teaching that there was death before the Fall weakens the reason for the cross. If the penalty was only spiritual separation from God (spiritual death), why did Jesus not come down from the cross when He cried, 'It is finished!' (John 19:30)? It is evident that the answer carries a major truth: Christ paid the price for sin and went through physical death and resurrection so that those who believe might have a new resurrected physical body on the day of His return when 'we shall all be changed' (see 1 Cor. 15:51–55). Christ's physical death is connected with the origin of physical death in the garden of Eden.

There are a number of other modern commentaries on the text. A straightforward and easy-to-read commentary is *The Book of Origins* by Philip Eveson (Evangelical Press, 2013), though Eveson is equivocal concerning whether the days are really ordinary solar days.[2] Another dealing with creation issues and which complements this work is *The Six Days of Genesis* by Paul F. Taylor (Master Books, 2007). Other very helpful books are *The Genesis Record* (Grand Rapids, 1976) and *The Defender's Study Bible* (Thomas Nelson, 2005), both by Henry Morris. The *MacArthur Study Bible* also has very helpful notes on Genesis.

Another excellent book that has recently been published—William Vandoodewaard, *The Quest for the Historical Adam* (Reformation

Heritage Books, 2015)—is an exhaustive study showing the decline in belief in Scripture in evangelical seminaries in the last hundred years, and the battleground that has therefore emerged between the resurgence of those seeking to stand for biblical inerrancy and those seeking to accommodate the evolutionary viewpoint and insert a reading into Genesis which the text does not support.

It is in the midst of this confusion in theological circles that this commentary makes a case for reading the Scripture in general, and Genesis in particular, in a straightforward way, without the tortuous positioning of arguments trying to accommodate evolutionary sophistry. It has been the position of the evangelical church down the centuries that on all the major doctrines Scripture is clear. We call this the doctrine of the perspicuity (clarity) of Scripture: that there is no doctrine in Scripture that needs extraneous sources to justify it. So when it comes to creation and the subject of origins, Genesis with the whole of Scripture is all one needs. It was said of Tyndale that he retorted to a clergyman who resisted his translation of the Bible into English, 'I will cause a boy that driveth the plough to know more of the Scriptures than thou dost.' And that was the mark of the Protestant Reformation: that though learning has its place, nevertheless it must not be positioned *above* Scripture.

The right way to approach Scripture is to be humble before it. Scripture examines us, not the other way round: 'For the word of God is living and powerful, and sharper than any two-edged sword, piercing even to the division of soul and spirit, and of joints and marrow, and is a discerner of the thoughts and intents of the heart' (Heb. 4:12). Consequently, in our approach to Genesis we must come humbly before it and allow the Scriptures themselves to reveal their amazing truth, rather than seek to use sources outside Scripture to interpret the text.

A major principle in understanding key passages such as Genesis 1–11 is to recognize that the Scriptures are like a tapestry, with themes running all the way through, so to understand one passage we often need to read other passages where key principles are given as to how to understand the passage in question. This is certainly true for the first few chapters of Genesis, concerning whose interpretation many New Testament Scriptures can be brought to bear. We note that major doctrines find their roots in the early chapters of Genesis and are developed further in the rest of Scripture, particularly in the New Testament. They include the following:

- The Trinity was involved in creation (Gen. 1:2; 1:26), with Christ pre-eminent (Col. 1:12–18; John 1:3).
- Adam and Eve were made at the beginning of creation (Gen. 1–2; Matt. 19:4).
- Man is made in the image of God and is different from the animals (Gen. 1:27; 1 Cor. 11:7).
- Woman was not made from dust as Adam was, but from part of man (Gen. 2; 1 Tim. 2:13–15).
- Marriage is defined as being between one man and one woman (Gen. 2:23; Matt. 19:4–5; Eph. 5:31).
- Man is given dominion and authority over the animal kingdom (so Noah was commanded to take two of every air-breathing land animal into the ark, Gen. 6:19).
- Evil originated with Satan (Gen. 3; John 8:44).
- Adam brought suffering and death upon the whole human race; there was no death beforehand (Rom. 5; 1 Cor. 15).
- Sin also brings hardship in work for man and in childbearing for women (1 Tim. 2:14–15).
- Blood sacrifice is essential to atone for sin (Gen. 3:21; 4:4; Heb. 9:22)
- The Seed of the woman would come and bruise the serpent's head: Christ would be born of a virgin (Gen. 3:15; Isa. 7:14; Luke 2).
- Clothing is needed as a direct consequence of the Fall (Gen. 3:21; 1 Tim. 2:9).
- The worldwide Flood was a type of the final judgement to come (Luke 17:26–27). Just as the Second Coming of Christ will be universal, concerning all people, so the Flood was universal, concerning the whole world (Gen. 6–9; Luke 17:20–27; 2 Peter 3).

I encourage you to read other reliable books which look in detail at the theological and scientific issues raised by adopting a plain, straightforward approach to Genesis (such as my *Genesis For Today* and Douglas Kelly's *Creation and Change* (Mentor, 2004). The following paragraphs summarize the main arguments for taking the position commonly called Young Earth Creation:

(1) The theology of death being the consequence of sin is linked to

the theology of the atonement taught in the New Testament—notably in Romans 5 and 1 Corinthians 15. As explained above, the theistic evolution position (which seeks to accommodate evolution within Scripture) attempts unsuccessfully to have pre-Adamic creatures evolving (and physically dying) before Adam and the Fall of Adam. Consequently, its proponents try to suggest that Adam died only spiritually after the Fall. But why did Jesus die physically on the cross if the penalty for sin was only spiritual death? Spiritual death was a penalty Christ took on the cross when He was separated from His Father and bore the full wrath of Almighty God upon Himself. As He suffered in the final three hours of darkness on the cross, He cried out, 'My God, My God, why have You forsaken Me?' (Matt. 27:46). This was the blackest moment as Christ, still alive, was bearing my sin, such that God the Father (usually addressed by Christ as 'Abba') was now distant from His Son, who endured the anger of God against Him. Shortly after this, Christ then cried out, 'It is finished!' (John 19:30). This is one word in the Greek: *teteleste*—'Complete!' If the penalty was only spiritual death, why did Christ go further and dismiss His spirit from His body in John 19:30? The reason is that there was still the physical death (separation of the spirit from the body) to go through in order to buy all those who believe in Christ the right to a new body on the last day. None of this makes sense if the penalty of sin were only a spiritual death and not also a physical death. The gospel is inextricably connected to creation and the Fall.

(2) The exposition of Genesis 1 in other New Testament Scriptures shows that the *agent* of creation was Christ (John 1; Col. 1) and the *agency* was His spoken word. The *same person* with the *same agency* is recorded on many occasions performing miracles of healing, resurrection (e.g. John 11:43, 'Lazarus, come forth!') or even commanding inanimate wind and water to be still (e.g. Mark 4:39). Most of the miracles of Christ were performed with immediate effect. The implication is that the creation events of the first week were also immediate in effect.

(3) The study of the Hebrew word *yom* used for the 'days' of the creation week shows that when the word is used elsewhere in the Old Testament with evening and morning, or with evening alone or morning alone, it always means a normal twenty-four-hour day. Though the word *yom* can (as in English) be used to mean an indefinite period (just as we

might say, 'The day of George Washington', meaning the period under the first President of the United States), the use of 'evening and morning' in Genesis 1 precludes this. A classic example is 1 Samuel 17:16, when Goliath is challenging the armies of Israel to give him a man to fight; the text states that he 'drew near and presented himself forty days, morning and evening'. The context and the use of 'morning and evening' shows that this means ordinary days. Also, the use of numerals with the word 'day' invariably means that the word 'day' is to be taken to mean the ordinary solar day. Thus there are no grounds for supposing that one should interpret the word 'day' any differently in Genesis 1.

(4) There are key verses outside Genesis 1 which refer to a creation of six literal days. In particular, the Sabbath command in Exodus 20:8–11 specifically gives the reason for the week as being because 'in six days the LORD made the heavens and earth, the sea, and all that is in them, and rested the seventh day'. This is repeated in Exodus 31:17: 'in six days the LORD made the heavens and the earth, and on the seventh day He rested and was refreshed.' This statement not only underlines a creation of six literal days, but also emphasizes that all the created order (including the universe of stars made on the fourth day) was made in the creation week.

It is the purpose of this commentary not to look at all the book of Genesis, but rather to consider the most attacked part, Genesis 1–11, which is the major historical timeline from the creation of the universe through Adam to Noah, and on through the worldwide Flood to Abraham.

Notes

1 **Denis Alexander,** Creation or Evolution: Do We Have to Choose? (Oxford: Lion, 2008), p. 275.
2 See p. 30 of **Eveson's** book.

Genesis 1 The creation of the light, the expanse separating water above and beneath, the land, trees and plants, the sun, moon and stars, the fish and the birds, land animals and man.

Genesis 2 The detail of the creation of man, his dominion over the animals, the creation of woman.

Genesis 3 The Fall of man, the serpent, the curse on the ground, the entry of suffering and death into Adam and Eve's experience.

Genesis 4 Cain's murder of Abel, Cain's descendants, birth of Seth.

Genesis 5 Descendants of Seth down to Noah.

Genesis 6–9 The building of the ark, the saving of the animals and Noah's family, the worldwide Flood, and the rainbow promise.

Genesis 10 The table of the nations and the early descendants after the Flood from Shem, Ham and Japheth.

Genesis 11 The tower of Babel, the descendants of Shem down to Abraham.

Chapter 1

1 In the beginning God created the heavens and the earth.

2 The earth was without form, and void; and darkness was on the face of the deep. And the Spirit of God was hovering over the face of the waters.

3 Then God said, 'Let there be light'; and there was light.

4 And God saw the light, that it was good; and God divided the light from the darkness.

5 God called the light Day, and the darkness He called Night. So the evening and the morning were the first day.

6 Then God said, 'Let there be a firmament in the midst of the waters, and let it divide the waters from the waters.'

7 Thus God made the firmament, and divided the waters which were under the firmament from the waters which were above the firmament; and it was so

8 And God called the firmament Heaven. So the evening and the morning were the second day.

1:1 *In the beginning God … earth.* The beginning of time; the beginning of space; the beginning of matter. This opening verse of the Bible shows that the essence of the universe is time, space and matter, and that all came from Him and are under His control. *Elohim* ('God'), which is in the plural form, indicates that the Trinity was there right at the beginning, at creation. The word translated 'create' is the Hebrew *bara*, which means to create something new, and here it has the sense of 'to create out of nothing'. Though some would argue that verses 1–2 are a prelude and not part of the creation week, a comparison of this verse with Exodus 20:11 as well as with Genesis 1:14–17 leads us to a different conclusion. In Exodus 20:11 God specifically records, 'For in six days the LORD made the heavens and the earth, the sea, and all that is in them'; and the word translated 'the heavens' (Heb. *samaiym*, a word implying the dual 'heavens') is the same as that used in 1:1, the opening verse of the Bible, and again in 1:14 and 1:17, where we are told that God placed the stars in 'the firmament of the heavens'. In verses 6–8 we see that this firmament was an entity (space or expanse) which was specifically created and that the stars were placed in it. Thus the firmament and the stars are very much part of the six-day creation. Once we realize that space was part of the creation, any sense of a primeval universe before the six-day acts of God's voice, based on verses 1–2, becomes untenable. Verses 1–2 are therefore a summary of what God did in the creation week, a summary of what is going to be described in detail in the six days which are unfolded to the reader in the following verses.

1:2 *Without form, and void*. Some have tried to argue for an earlier spoilt creation made void. But the words *tohu wa bohu* are well translated as 'without form, and void'. The word *tohu* is used in Job 26:7: 'He stretches out the north over empty [*tohu*] space.' It simply means just as it says: 'without anything else there'. The phrase is also used in Jeremiah 4:23: 'I beheld the earth, and indeed it was without form, and void; and the heavens, they had no light.' In that passage Jeremiah is saying that the nation of Israel is without life and dead, just as the original world was. The gap theorists maintain that at the beginning, the early earth was spoilt by the devil. This is based on a wrong understanding that 'without form, and void' means that some corruption took place. However, a key verse is Isaiah 45:18: '[The LORD] formed it [the earth] to be inhabited.' Isaiah shows that the earth was formed to be inhabited by people at the beginning, not millions (or indeed thousands) of years later. Genesis 1:31 also conflicts with that view, since this verse states that all that God had made was very good. Before Genesis 1:31 there was nothing out of place on the earth, in the universe or in the spiritual realm of creation.

1:2 *The Spirit of God was hovering over the face of the waters.* Wherever God is acting, His Spirit is there. The Trinity is evident throughout this chapter. See verse 26, where again God in His plurality creates man in His image. The Spirit of God 'was hovering'—the Hebrew word can also be translated 'moved' or 'was brooding upon'. There is a sense of great movement and of imminent action. The 'waters' are what God started with; as discussed above under 1:1, because of the statement in Exodus 20:11 we can see that these waters were part of the creation week. Initially this is all there was; not even space, in which the stars would later be placed, was yet made.

1:3 *Let there be light.* This is the first recorded creating act of God; notice that it was by the *spoken* word of God. This is the pattern of creation in Genesis 1, and from John 1:3 and Colossians 1:12–18 we know that this was Christ speaking everything into existence with the same power He displayed in the many miracles He performed. His same power will bring the world abruptly to an end (1 Thes. 4:16; 2 Peter 3:7–10).

There is no evolutionary process implied here. The creation of light was profound—firstly, physically, since it is likely that this was the creation of the whole electromagnetic spectrum, which is fundamental to the very essence of physical existence itself. Without electromagnetism, nothing could exist in the material world. Secondly, spiritually, this creation shows the nature of God, for 'God is light and in Him is no darkness at all' (1 John 1:5). In Hebrews 1:3 Christ is described as 'the brightness of His glory and the express image of His person'. The radiance of the Father is the glory of God, which is Christ Himself. So the Shekinah glory of the Old Testament was none other than Christ, leading the Israelites through the wilderness in the cloudy pillar by day and the pillar of fire by night (Exod. 13:20–22). John 17:22 speaks of the glory that God the Father had given to Christ now being given to us. The thought is followed through in 2 Corinthians 4:6, where Paul draws an analogy between the creation of light and the regeneration of the believer. In both cases it is the action of Christ. Think of it: the phrase 'who has shone in our hearts' is stating that the wonder of being born again by God's Holy Spirit (who is elsewhere called the Spirit of Christ: see Rom. 8:9; 1 Peter 1:11) is equal to the power displayed on the first day of creation. That is surely awesome!

1:4 *It was good.* This is another repeated phrase—see comment below on 1:31. Here the 'it was good' shows that even the inanimate creation is not ethically neutral. God pronounces the light 'good'. In 1 Corinthians 14:33 we read, 'God is not the author of confusion.'

1:5 *God called the light Day, and the darkness he called Night.* All that is needed is a rotating globe and a directional aspect to the light to produce day and night. We cannot say, as others suggest, that the sun was already in place, since we know that the sun was not made till the fourth day. Jeremiah 4:23 alludes to the fact that the world was originally in darkness. So what was the light? It could have emanated from God Himself; recall that Christ shone with His own light on the mount of transfiguration (Matt. 17), and Revelation 21:23 states that the New

Jerusalem 'had no need of the sun ... for the glory of God illuminated it. The Lamb [Christ] is its light.'

1:6–8 *Firmament.* The Hebrew word *raqiya* has the sense of 'expanse' and is a very important concept. It was not just the sky, since God calls the firmament 'Heaven' (v. 8) and the stars are put in the firmament (v. 14). This is the expanse which God stretched out (Job 9:8; Ps. 104:2; Isa. 40:22; 42:5; 44:24; 45:12; 48:13; 51:13; Jer. 10:12; Zech. 12:1). The stretching may have happened on this second day; however, it is more likely that it happened on the fourth day, after the stars were made. This firmament was not, therefore, just empty space. In recent years, physicists have begun to realize that space is indeed an entity which may have energy in it, and that in some sense (still waiting to be properly understood) it is part of the physical order and essential for anything else to exist. The Bible makes it plain that indeed *raqiya* is a most important part of creation. Though early thinkers thought of the heavens as a solid dome carrying the stars along with it (which the rise of modern astronomy later showed to be false), the concept of an entity in which the stars are placed is clearly presented when it comes to the final *end* of the universe, when the Lord will collapse the stars: 'the stars will fall from heaven' (Matt. 24:29); 'the heavens are the work of Your hands ... Like a cloak You will fold them up' (Heb. 1:10, 12, quoting Ps. 102:25–26).

---

9 Then God said, 'Let the waters under the heavens be gathered together into one place, and let the dry land appear'; and it was so.

10 And God called the dry land Earth, and the gathering together of the waters He called Seas. And God saw that it was good.

11 Then God said, 'Let the earth bring forth grass, the herb that yields seed, and the fruit tree that yields fruit according to its kind, whose seed is in itself, on the earth'; and it was so.

12 And the earth brought forth grass, the herb that yields seed according to its kind, and the tree that yields fruit, whose seed is in itself according to its kind. And God saw that it was good.

13 So the evening and the morning were the third day.

14 Then God said, 'Let there be lights in the firmament of the heavens to divide the day from the

night; and let them be for signs and seasons, and for days and years;

15 and let them be for lights in the firmament of the heavens to give light on the earth'; and it was so.

16 Then God made two great lights: the greater light to rule the day, and the lesser light to rule the night. He made the stars also.

17 God set them in the firmament of the heavens to give light on the earth,

18 and to rule over the day and over the night, and to divide the light from the darkness. And God saw that it was good.

19 So the evening and the morning were the fourth day.

20 Then God said, 'Let the waters abound with an abundance of living creatures, and let birds fly above the earth across the face of the firmament of the heavens.'

21 So God created great sea creatures and every living thing that moves, with which the waters abounded, according to their kind, and every winged bird according to its kind. And God saw that it was good.

22 And God blessed them, saying, 'Be fruitful and multiply, and fill the waters in the seas, and let birds multiply on the earth.'

23 So the evening and the morning were the fifth day.

24 Then God said, 'Let the earth bring forth the living creature according to its kind: cattle and creeping thing and beast of the earth, each according to its kind'; and it was so.

25 And God made the beast of the earth according to its kind, cattle according to its kind, and everything that creeps on the earth according to its kind. And God saw that it was good.

1:9 *Let the waters under the heavens be gathered together into one place, and let the dry land appear.* The land appears; and note that some New Testament verses refer to the explicit nature of this separation: 2 Peter 3:5 describes 'the earth standing out of water and in the water', which confirms the text of Genesis 1:9 that the dry land appeared in such a manner that some was still under water and some above.

1:11 *Whose seed is in itself.* The first living things are made: plants and trees with 'seed in [themselves]'. The mark of living things is that they can generate offspring.

1:14–19 *Lights in the firmament.* The momentous creation of the sun, the moon and the stars. This is so often dismissed by liberal and even evangelical scholars, but the text is clear. God did not make the stars until the fourth day. The light of the sun, moon and stars takes over from the light source of the first three days. The stretching out of the heavens (see comment above on vv. 6–8) may well have occurred after the placing of the stars and galaxies.

What is staggering is the phrase at the end of verse 16: 'He made the stars also.' Psalm 147:4 and Isaiah 40:26 state that 'He calls them all *by name*' (emphasis added). There are an estimated 200 billion stars in the Milky Way galaxy alone—that is, an estimated 2×10^{11}. There are an estimated 100 billion galaxies in the universe, so the number of stars is at least 2×10^{22}. If a computer were observing 10 million per second, it would take 63 million years to count all the stars! Such is the power of the Almighty! Abraham is told in Genesis 15:5, 'Count the stars if you are able to number them …' The stars are the work of God's fingers (Ps. 8:3), but salvation is the work of His right hand (Ps. 98:1). Remember also that the stars will fall from heaven when it comes to the final judgement (Isa. 13:10; Joel 3:15; Matt. 24:29; Rev. 6:13). That will not be a slow evolutionary event either! The universe will be 'folded up' 'like a cloak' (Ps. 102:26; Heb. 1:10–12).

1:20–23 *God created great sea creatures and every living thing that moves, with which the waters abounded, according to their kind, and every winged bird according to its kind*. Notice that both the swimming creatures as well as the flying creatures (birds, bats and flying insects) all came before the land creatures. Evolution would have us believe that 'convergent evolution' produced flight at different stages of development—Carboniferous dragonflies, then pterodactyls in the Jurassic age, and finally flying mammals (bats) and birds in the Tertiary. The truth is that these were all made on day 5 of creation.

1:21 *Great sea creatures*. The 'great sea creatures' (or 'great whales', KJV) are singled out. They seem to be different from both fish and sea-going reptiles (like crocodiles). The word here translated 'sea creatures' is *tanniyn*, which elsewhere in the New King James Version is translated in a variety of ways: as 'sea creature' (Ps. 148:7), 'sea serpent' (Job 7:12; Ps. 74:13), 'monster' (Ezek. 29:3; 32:2; Jer. 51:34), 'serpent' (Exod. 7:9–10, 12; Deut. 32:33; Neh. 2:13; Ps. 91:13; Isa. 51:9), 'jackal' (Job 30:29; Ps. 44:19; Isa. 13:22; 34:13; 35:7;

43:20; Jer. 9:11; 10:22; 14:6; 49:33; 51:37; Lam. 4:3; Micah 1:8) and 'reptile' (Isa. 27:1). This variation in translation in the New King James Version is not as consistent as in the King James Version, which for the above references translates *tanniyn* as 'dragon' except in Job 7:12 and Ezekiel 32:2, where it is translated 'whale'; Exodus 7:9–10, 12, where it is translated 'serpent'; and Lamentations 4:3, where it is translated 'sea monster'.

'Dragon' (as in KJV) is likely to be a better translation of *tanniyn* since in Isaiah 27:1 there is a reference to 'Leviathan' (*liwyatan*) and 'serpent' (*nahas*) as well as *tanniyn* (translated in the NKJV as 'reptile' and in the KJV as 'dragon'). Psalm 74:13–14 also has 'Leviathan' with *tanniyn* (translated in the NKJV as 'sea serpent' and in the KJV as 'dragon'). From the context of these two passages, all three words seem to be referring to large creatures (in a similar way to Job 41 describing Leviathan), so many think that this could be a reference to a grouping of large sea-going dinosaurs (plesiosaurs).

It is possible that the King James Version translation 'whales' in Genesis 1:21 is correct, or that whales are included in the meaning of *tanniyn*. These sea-going mammals (giving birth to live young) can be massive. The blue whale is the largest creature known at 30 metres in length and an immense 180 tonnes in weight. The cetaceans (whales and dolphins/porpoises) are unique in their blow-hole structure for breathing.

1:24 *Cattle and creeping thing and beast of the earth, each according to its kind.* The sixth day sees the land animals created. The first group 'cattle' (Heb. *behema*) literally means 'dumb brute' and is translated *tetrapoda* in the Greek Septuagint. Most commentators take the view that this refers to the creatures that can be domesticated as livestock. The second kind referred to as 'creeping thing' (Heb. *remes*) could be reptiles (the Septuagint translates this as *erpeta*, 'reptiles') such as crocodiles and lizards as well as insects that move close to the ground. The third group translated as 'beast of the earth' (Heb. *chay erets*) has the sense of 'life of the earth'. It would seem that these creatures are the wild animals as against the ones in the first group, which can be domesticated.

1:25 *God saw that it was good.* This is the sixth occurrence of the total of seven pronouncements by God concerning the goodness of creation. These are found in 1:4 (day 1: light), 1:10 (day 3: separation of water and earth), 1:12 (day 3: herbs and trees), 1:18 (day 4: sun, moon and stars), 1:21 (day 5: sea-going and flying creatures), 1:25 (day 6: land animals) and 1:31 (day 6: man and all that God has made). There can be no doubt that God made an originally perfect creation.

---

26 Then God said, 'Let Us make man in Our image, according to Our likeness; let them have dominion over the fish of the sea, over the birds of the air, and over the cattle, over all the earth and over every creeping thing that creeps on the earth.'

27 So God created man in His own image; in the image of God He created him; male and female He created them.

28 Then God blessed them, and God said to them, 'Be fruitful and multiply; fill the earth and subdue it; have dominion over the fish of the sea, over the birds of the air, and over every living thing that moves on the earth.'

29 And God said, 'See, I have given you every herb that yields seed which is on the face of all the earth, and every tree whose fruit yields seed; to you it shall be for food.

30 Also, to every beast of the earth, to every bird of the air, and to everything that creeps on the earth, in which there is life, I have given every green herb for food'; and it was so.

31 Then God saw everything that He had made, and indeed it was very good. So the evening and the morning were the sixth day.

1:26 *Let Us make man in Our image, according to Our likeness.* The plurality of the Godhead is taught in a number of places in Genesis 1: in 1:1, 'In the beginning God', where the word translated 'God' is *Elohim* (plural); in 1:2, 'the Spirit of God was hovering over the face of the waters', which shows that God's Spirit is active; and in 1:26, 'Let *Us* make man …' (emphasis added). It is significant that when it comes to the creation of man the plurality of God is stressed, since *relationship* lies at the heart of God's very being; so man is created in relationship first with God and later with his wife, Eve. Man cannot be defined without reference to God. The verb 'make' here is *asah*, which has the sense of 'prepare'.

1:27 *Male and female He created them.* The first mention of female is in the context of both man and woman being created in God's image; and here the word 'created' is *bara*, which has the sense of 'creation from new'. There is no development from existing creatures as taught by evolutionary sophistry.

1:28 *Be fruitful and multiply; fill the earth and subdue it.* The dominion mandate to man is clear. He is not from the animals. He is different from them and made in God's image, with delegated authority over the world and the animals.

1:29 *I have given you every herb that yields seed … to you it shall be for food.* Man at this stage is vegetarian. After the Flood man is allowed to eat meat; and Genesis 9:3—'Every moving thing that lives shall be food for you. I have given you all things, *even as the green herbs*' (emphasis added)—refers back to the command at creation.

1:30 *To every beast … I have given every green herb for food.* The animals were vegetarian also. There was no animal death before the Fall of man. Many find difficulty with this concept. However, it has been shown that lions can live on a vegetable and fruit diet—for example, a lioness in Africa in the period 1946–1955.[1] Sharp teeth do not necessarily mean that animals must always be carnivorous. The giant panda is a classic example; it has sharp teeth and yet eats bamboo.

1:31 *Then God saw everything that He had made, and indeed it was very good.* The seventh and final statement that all was good. There was nothing out of place in all creation. No predator killing prey. No death and destruction of any kind. There is an allusion to this perfection in Isaiah 11:6: 'The wolf also shall dwell with the lamb, the leopard shall lie down with the young goat.' Whatever one's view as to whether or not this is a literal picture of the future state, it is clear that Isaiah's statement must be referring to no killing in the animal kingdom in the initial pre-Fall perfect creation. Neither was anything out of place in the extraterrestrial universe—the planets, stars and galaxies. This statement must include the angels, since these are also created beings. Consequently the fall of Satan must have occurred after day 6 of creation.

Note

1 **David Catchpoole,** 'The Lion That Wouldn't Eat Meat', *Creation* 22 (22–23 March 2000): 22–23; available at http://creation.com/the-lion-that-wouldnt-eat-meat.

Chapter 2

1 Thus the heavens and the earth, and all the host of them, were finished.

2 And on the seventh day God ended His work which He had done, and He rested on the seventh day from all His work which He had done.

3 Then God blessed the seventh day and sanctified it, because in it He rested from all His work which God had created and made.

2:3 *God blessed the seventh day and sanctified it.* There is no doubt that the rest on the seventh day is a creation ordinance and thus is to be regarded as a day not only for the Israelites later but for all people. It is significant that most of the Ten Commandments were known as principles before they were given by God at Sinai. The seventh day was a day when God Himself rested, not because He needed to, but as an example. The important issue is keeping one day in seven, though good reasons are given concerning the change of day by Jonathan Edwards in *The Perpetuity and Change of the Sabbath*.[1]

---

4 This is the history of the heavens and the earth when they were created, in the day that the LORD God made the earth and the heavens,

5 before any plant of the field was in the earth and before any herb of the field had grown. For the LORD God had not caused it to rain on the earth, and there was no man to till the ground;

6 but a mist went up from the earth and watered the whole face of the ground.

7 And the LORD God formed man of the dust of the ground, and breathed into his nostrils the breath of life; and man became a living being.

8 The LORD God planted a garden eastward in Eden, and there He put the man whom He had formed.

9 And out of the ground the LORD God made every tree grow that is pleasant to the sight and good for

food. The tree of life was also in the midst of the garden, and the tree of the knowledge of good and evil.

10 Now a river went out of Eden to water the garden, and from there it parted and became four riverheads.

11 The name of the first is Pishon; it is the one which skirts the whole land of Havilah, where there is gold.

12 And the gold of that land is good. Bdellium and the onyx stone are there.

13 The name of the second river is Gihon; it is the one which goes around the whole land of Cush.

14 The name of the third river is Hiddekel; it is the one which goes toward the east of Assyria. The fourth river is the Euphrates.

15 Then the LORD God took the man and put him in the garden of Eden to tend and keep it.

16 And the LORD God commanded the man, saying, 'Of every tree of the garden you may freely eat;

17 but of the tree of the knowledge of good and evil you shall not eat, for in the day that you eat of it you shall surely die.'

18 And the LORD God said, 'It is not good that man should be alone; I will make him a helper comparable to him.'

19 Out of the ground the LORD God formed every beast of the field and every bird of the air, and brought them to Adam to see what he would call them. And whatever Adam called each living creature, that was its name.

20 So Adam gave names to all cattle, to the birds of the air, and to every beast of the field. But for Adam there was not found a helper comparable to him.

21 And the LORD God caused a deep sleep to fall on Adam, and he slept; and He took one of his ribs, and closed up the flesh in its place.

22 Then the rib which the LORD God had taken from man He made into a woman, and He brought her to the man.

23 And Adam said: 'This is now bone of my bones and flesh of my flesh; she shall be called Woman, because she was taken out of Man.'

24 Therefore a man shall leave his father and mother and be joined to his wife, and they shall become one flesh.

25 And they were both naked, the man and his wife, and were not ashamed.

2:4 *This is the history* (or 'These are the generations', KJV). Many regard this phrase which occurs throughout Genesis as the narrator's introduction to a new section. The Hebrew word is *toledoth* (what is 'born' or 'generated') and it is used in the following verses: 2:4 (heavens and earth), 5:1 (Adam), 6:9 (Noah), 10:1 (sons of Noah), 11:10 (Shem), 11:27 (Terah), 25:12 (Ishmael), 25:19 (Isaac), 36:1 (Esau), 36:9 (Esau again), and 37:2 (Jacob).

2:4 *In the day that the LORD God made the earth and the heavens.* The use of the word 'day' in this verse is a good example of where it does not mean a twenty-four-hour day. It has no numeral attached to it and there is no mention of evening and morning. The context shows that it is referring to the period when all the heavens and the earth were made—the period of six days when the whole of creation took place.

2:5–6 *The LORD God had not caused it to rain on the earth … a mist went up from the earth.* Certainly this indicates that there was no violent rainfall before the Flood. It may even be that there was literally no rain at all. How could that be? The key is verse 6, which states, 'a mist went up from the earth.' Though Hebrew scholars are not sure as to the exact meaning of *ed* (translated 'mist'), the context suggests this rendering or possibly a spring which watered the ground. Thus we can be sure that before the Flood there was a good watering system using rivers and a dew arising by condensation. After the Flood God brought the rainbow as a sign that He would never flood the earth again (9:13), so we know there was a great difference between the hydrological systems before and after the Flood.

2:7 *The LORD God formed man.* This is not a different creation account. Genesis 1 is the grand overarching statement of the big picture of creation, in which the main features of the creation week are summarized. Now the Lord homes in on the detail of the garden of Eden, the creation of man, and in particular the creation of Eve. It is rather like putting a magnifying glass on day 6 to highlight the climax of the creation week, which undoubtedly was the creation of man and woman.

2:7 *Of the dust of the ground.* The first man was not formed of creatures already made; he did not come from some kind of ape-man through a long evolutionary process. He was made from dust which God formed into Adam. The name 'Adam' is linked to the word *adamah*, meaning 'from the earth, ruddy', so his name is linked to his origin. The word translated 'formed' is from *yatsar*, which has the sense of 'framed', 'fashioned'.

2:7 *God … breathed into his nostrils the breath of life.* The life of man could never have arisen naturally; it came directly from the breath of God.

2:7 *Man became a living being* (lit. *chay*, 'living', *nephesh*, 'that which breathes'). Because he is made in God's image there is a direct action of God in his creation. God could have said, 'Let the dust bring forth a man' (in the same way as the Lord made the animals), but Adam is formed (Heb. *yatsar*, 'shaped') of the dust and then God breathes into him. As a consequence his life is more than an animal spirit.

2:8 *God planted a garden.* There is order and beauty in God's original creation, and all that man could need is provided for him.

2:9 *The tree of life was also in the midst of the garden.* The first mention of the tree of life. It is mentioned here at the beginning of creation, and significantly it is also mentioned at the end of Scripture in Revelation 22:2 and 22:14. How symbolic that our great Saviour, who is 'the way, the truth, and the life' (John 14:6), was nailed to a tree (though it was not called the tree of life) for our sins and took the weight of our punishment. Thus in the Gospels we also effectively have a tree of life: 'And as Moses lifted up the serpent in the wilderness, even so must the Son of Man be lifted up, that whoever believes in Him should not perish but have eternal life' (John 3:14–15).

2:9 *And the tree of the knowledge of good and evil.* Present also was the tree of the knowledge of good and evil. Note that this tree was not itself evil. It was the disobedience to God's command later concerning the tree which brought evil. God has knowledge of evil, and initially He created man not to have this knowledge. But man was not thus a robot: he had choice, and only in his pre-Fall condition did he have perfect liberty to do that which is good.

2:10 *A river went out of Eden.* There are four rivers which come out of the original Edenic river: Pishon, Gihon, Hiddekel and Euphrates. These mean respectively, 'Increase', 'Bursting forth', 'Rapid' and 'Fruitfulness'. These rivers are not the same as rivers with these names today since Eden was destroyed along with all the other original land mass at the worldwide Flood. So why do we still have a Euphrates river in the Middle East? The answer is that familiar names were used in the new world after the Flood in much the same way as place names in the US are often new versions of places in Europe and particularly England. For example, Manchester, New Hampshire, is named after the northern English city Manchester; and Birmingham, Alabama, is named after the English Midlands city Birmingham. Eden cannot be found at all in the present world, contrary to the thinking of authors such as Victor Pearce, who argues for Eden being in the present Middle East.[2] This is quite wrong. We need to recognize the force of 2 Peter 3:6: 'the world that then existed perished.' That past world before the Flood is irrevocably gone and was buried under thousands of feet of sediment.

2:11–14 *…where there is gold. And the gold of that land is good. Bdellium and the onyx stone are there.* Many have noted that verses 10–14 describe locations, lands, rivers and even the geology (gold and precious stones) in the present tense. It is rightly pointed out that the writer knew these locations and facts about them as being true in his day. To understand this, it is important to realize that, although the first five books (the Pentateuch, also called 'the Torah' by the Jews) are called the books of Moses, Moses did not write all of them. In particular, Genesis is a compilation of records that Moses evidently had access to. The creation records must have been communicated from God directly and were probably compiled by Adam. It is possible that Adam wrote the record of the lands and rivers described here in Genesis 2:10–14, which would explain why it is in the present tense and was transcribed as such. These writings, including the description of the lands and rivers coming from Eden, would have been passed down and treasured by the godly line— Adam to Seth, and down to Noah, then on from Noah to Shem, and then to Abraham, Isaac, Jacob and the children of Israel. Finally, these early writings were brought together by Moses as the first book of the Torah— Genesis.

2:15 *To tend and keep it.* Even in the pre-Fall world Adam had work to do. When again man is without sin in the new heavens and new earth to come, he will not be idle. Work only became a drudgery after the Fall.

2:16 *God commanded.* This is the first solemn charge that God gives to Adam. On the one hand, Adam can eat freely of all the trees in the garden …

2:17 *But of the tree of the knowledge of good and evil you shall not eat.* There is one tree from which he is not to eat. The negative command was a test of obedience but also a test of man's trust in God: that God knew what was right for man better than Adam did.

2:17 *In the day that you eat of it you shall surely die.* The warning and threat bring the first mention of death.

2:18 *It is not good that man should be alone.* Just as God is in eternal relationship as Father–Son–Holy Spirit, so man created in God's image should be in relationship with God and with fellow man. Supremely, Ephesians 5 teaches that marriage is a picture of Christ and the church.

2:19–20 *Whatever Adam called each living creature, that was its name. So Adam gave names to all cattle.* In 2:20 it says that he named explicitly the cattle, the birds of the air and the beasts of the field. We note two things: firstly, Adam was made with speech and the ability immediately to compare and make distinctions. Secondly, this feat of taxonomical naming of land and flying creatures would not have been so arduous, as he was not naming the sea creatures, and Adam's mind would have been sharp and bright. Morris estimates that around three thousand animals may have been named by Adam (*Defender's Study Bible*).

However, among all the creatures there was no helper for man. This underlines that woman's role is primarily to be a help to man. Though she is to bear children, that is not her primary role. Whether married or not, a woman will find her fulfilment before God primarily in the role of helper. Eveson aptly comments, 'She may be the last on the scene, but she is certainly not the least … She is as special and unique as the man … She shared the man's nature, but she did more: she complemented him. What he lacked she supplied, and what she lacked he supplied.'[3] The New Testament teaching in Titus 2:1–7 shows the working out of these two roles. Men are to learn to be sober and godly, but it is important to note that older women are to teach the young women also to be sober. The emphasis for women is to grow the true inner beauty of a meek and quiet spirit (1 Peter 3:4–5), rather than focus on outward adornment alone. Her focus is more naturally the home (Titus 2:5), but, like the young man, she also is to be taught systematically the Word of God—by older ladies (Titus 2:4). To neglect such ministry is to not prepare young women for their later fulfilment, and will lead to shallow motherhood when they in turn have children.

2:21–22 *Then the rib … He made into a woman, and He brought her to the man.* This is the climax of chapter 2 of Genesis. God has already stated that He created man, male and female, in 1:27, but here the Lord is explicitly telling us how He made Eve. It is not a different account but rather a beautiful detail in the tapestry of creation that He is showing us. The mode of creation of woman is vital in understanding the nature of woman, particularly within marriage. Woman has much that is common to man, but she was not made directly from dust. She was made from the rib of man (Heb. *tsela*, which in a number of places throughout the Old Testament is translated 'side' (e.g. Job 18:12) and in other places as 'chambers' (1 Kings 6:5b), 'beam' (1 Kings 7:3) and 'side chamber' (Ezek. 41:26, KJV)). Eve, unlike Adam, was not made from dust but from Adam. The word used here in Genesis 2:22 for 'made' with respect to woman is *banah* ('build')—not *asah* ('make', 'prepare'), as in 1:26; nor *bara* ('create new'), as in 1:27; nor *yatsar* ('formed', 'framed', 'fashioned'), as in 2:7. Here God is stressing that woman, though like man, is *built, intricately crafted and balanced* to complement man. Matthew Henry, in his devotional commentary, states that she was 'not made out of his head to rule over him, nor out of his feet to be trampled upon by him, but out of his side to be equal with him, under his arm to be protected, and near his heart to be beloved.'[4] Note that the New Testament comments on these verses also. Paul writes in 1 Timothy 2:13, 'Adam was formed first, then Eve'; and in 1 Corinthians 11:8–9 he says that the woman was made of the man and for the man. The order of creation shows that man is to lead, but 1 Corinthians 11:7 states that woman is the glory of man. The order of creation also shows that woman is the crown of the created order, and in particular is the crown of her husband. Another phrase of note is that God 'brought her to the man'. This shows that man should wait on God for His guidance in marriage.

2:23–25 *This is now bone of my bones and flesh of my flesh.* Adam's reaction is used as a spiritual parallel for the relationship of the church to Christ: 'For we are members of His body, of His flesh and of His bones' (Eph. 5:30). So in our marriages, husbands should love their wives as Christ loved the church, and wives should show reverence and be subject to their husbands as the church is to Christ.

The man is to 'leave his father and mother and be joined to ['cleave unto', KJV] his wife' (Gen. 2:24). This is a vital principle within marriage. There will still be respect and honour shown to parents, but there has to be a change from the old family relationships as a new family unit is set up. The man now cleaves to his wife, both sexually ('one flesh') and in terms of mutual support. Cleaving is associated with a covenant agreement (see, for instance, Deut. 10:20: 'to [God] shalt thou cleave, and swear by his name', KJV); and the Old Testament recognizes that marriage is a covenant agreement before God. Malachi 2:14 speaks of 'the wife of thy covenant' (KJV) and Proverbs 2:17 describes an unfaithful wife as one 'who forsakes the companion of her youth, and forgets the covenant of her God'.

In the pre-Fall state there was no clothing, and some have suggested there may have been a radiance, so that after the Fall, their awareness of their naked state was due to the removal of this radiance. Here in the pre-Fall state, intimacy and sexual joy are without shame, and Hebrews 13:4 teaches that even as fallen human beings, within matrimony, the bed is still undefiled. Sex in the right place is not evil.

Notes

1 *The Works of Jonathan Edwards,* Vol. 2, sermon 13 (Edinburgh: Banner of Truth, 1979), pp. 93–103; see also **J. C. Ryle,** 'Sabbath: A Day to Keep', http://www.fpcr.org/blue_banner_articles/ryle_sabbath.htm.

2 **Victor Pearce,** *Evidence for Truth: Science* (Guildford: Eagle, 1999).

3 **Eveson,** *Book of Origins.*

4 **Matthew Henry,** *Commentary on the Whole Bible,* Genesis 2:21–25; available at BibleGateway.com, https://www.biblegateway.com/resources/matthew-henry/toc.

Chapter 3

1 Now the serpent was more cunning than any beast of the field which the LORD God had made. And he said to the woman, 'Has God indeed said, "You shall not eat of every tree of the garden"?'

2 And the woman said to the serpent, 'We may eat the fruit of the trees of the garden;

3 but of the fruit of the tree which is in the midst of the garden, God has said, "You shall not eat it, nor shall you touch it, lest you die."'

4 Then the serpent said to the woman, 'You will not surely die.

5 For God knows that in the day you eat of it your eyes will be opened, and you will be like God, knowing good and evil.'

6 So when the woman saw that the tree was good for food, that it was pleasant to the eyes, and a tree desirable to make one wise, she took of its fruit and ate. She also gave to her husband with her, and he ate.

7 Then the eyes of both of them were opened, and they knew that they were naked; and they sewed fig leaves together and made themselves coverings.

3:1–6 *Has God indeed said, 'You shall not eat of every tree of the garden?'* The Fall of man is just as historical as the preceding two chapters. Without a literal Adam, a literal garden and a literal serpent, there is no reason to believe in a literal Christ, a literal cross and a literal resurrection. The theology of Romans 5 and 1 Corinthians 15 in this regard is inescapable. These are real historical events. Redemption in and through Christ and His cross is predicated upon a real historical Fall of man in the garden of Eden. The woman should not have engaged in conversation with the serpent. This was an unnatural occurrence. Animals do not generally talk, and Eve should have sought out Adam, to whom the command not to take the fruit of the tree of the knowledge of good and evil had originally been given. By heeding the serpent she moved away from Adam's authority over her.

She first *listened* to the serpent's voice and the questioning of God's word. The question of the devil, 'Has God indeed said …?' is the first question in the Bible and shows the devil's nature. John 8:44 says, 'he is a liar and the father of it.'

She then, secondly, *conversed* with the serpent. She is now being drawn into his deceit, for she answers his question in verses 2–3 by restating the command concerning the trees. She should not have conversed with him; Hezekiah explicitly told his people not to answer Rabshakeh in 2 Kings 18:36. We note that she adds the phrase 'nor shall you touch it' to God's original words to Adam concerning the tree of the knowledge of good and evil. It is a tendency of us all to misquote or add to Scripture, which we should not do (Deut. 4:2; Rev. 22:18–19). Having now drawn her into his web of deceit, the serpent now states a defiant and bold lie—'You will not surely die'—in direct contradiction to what God has said to Adam. As Zodhiates states in his commentary, 'Satan did not attempt to explain why they would not die; he merely affirmed it! And he said it so convincingly that Eve believed it.'[1] Then the devil arrogantly dares to suggest a motive for God's stipulation concerning the tree of the knowledge of good and evil: 'For God knows that … your eyes will be opened, and you will be like God.' This no doubt alludes to why he himself rebelled against God earlier: he wanted to be like God (Isa. 14:12–13).

Eve's conversing with the serpent brings her to the precipice of disaster, for she now *conceives* evil in her own heart. The seed of the enemy has lingered long enough to germinate in her soul. The progression within the mind is by far the most dangerous part of sin, before the act of disobedience is actually engaged in. Sin begins in the heart, as the Lord states directly in Matthew 15:11: 'what comes out of the mouth, this defiles a man'; and the apostle warns us in James 1:15, 'when desire has conceived, it gives birth to sin; and sin, when it is full-grown, brings forth death.' The thinking of the possibility first germinated in her heart, and then she *looked* and 'saw that the tree was good for food, that it was pleasant to the eyes, and a tree desirable to make one wise'. By the time she looked, she was over the cliff. The seed of evil was doing its work. She *desired*, and she *took*. The devil no longer needed to tempt Adam directly, for he knew Eve would influence her husband to do the same. Adam's sin comes right at the end of verse 6: 'She also gave to her husband with her, and he ate.' Paul gives us further insight in 1 Timothy 2:14: 'And Adam was not deceived …' Adam knew what he was doing, whereas Eve was tricked by the deceit of the devil. Thus from 1 Timothy 2:14 we know that Adam took the fruit wittingly; he knew it was from the tree of the knowledge of good and evil, and he rebelled against God's command.

3:7 *Then the eyes of both of them were opened.* There was an immediate effect of sin: they suddenly realized their vulnerability. If they had had a covering before (as mentioned above, some have suggested a radiance like that of Christ, Moses and Elijah in Matt. 17 on the mount of transfiguration), it was now gone. If it was not a physical effect before, they certainly were now aware that they were naked. This was physical awareness, but it spoke volumes regarding what had happened spiritually. Genesis 2:17 states, '… in the day that you eat of it you shall surely die'. Something had died. Death is separation, and their souls, which previously had always had communion with God's Spirit, were now cut off. Spiritual death had come in ('dead in trespasses and sins', Eph. 2:1) immediately. Physical death (separation of soul from body) would come nine hundred or so years later to Adam.

As with all sinners, their first thought was to cover their sin up. They were aware of their physical nakedness. The reality of what the devil had led them into now became all too apparent. The devil will lead man into nakedness spiritually and will often also lead men and women to physical immodesty. Adam and Eve immediately sewed fig leaves together to cover up their sin—but their inward vulnerability and nakedness before God could not be hidden. God knew.

---

8 And they heard the sound of the LORD God walking in the garden in the cool of the day, and Adam and his wife hid themselves from the presence of the LORD God among the trees of the garden.

9 Then the LORD God called to Adam and said to him, 'Where are you?'

10 So he said, 'I heard Your voice in the garden, and I was afraid because I was naked; and I hid myself.'

11 And He said, 'Who told you that you were naked? Have you eaten

from the tree of which I commanded you that you should not eat?' 12 Then the man said, 'The woman whom You gave to be with me, she gave me of the tree, and I ate.'

13 And the LORD God said to the woman, 'What is this you have done?' The woman said, 'The serpent deceived me, and I ate.'

3:8 *Adam and his wife hid themselves from the presence of the LORD God.* The first consequence of their sin was that they tried to *cover themselves* with fig leaves. But the next consequence was that they tried to *hide themselves* from the presence of God. We notice that 'they heard the sound of the LORD God walking in the garden'. Clearly it had been God's practice to seek out fellowship with Adam and Eve in the cool of each day. This shows two things: firstly, that God's presence was visible in a body walking in the garden. This is similar to the appearance of God to Abraham in Genesis 18 with two angels, and most commentators would see such as examples of a theophany (pre-incarnation appearance of the Lord Jesus Christ). Secondly, it also shows the close communion that Adam enjoyed with God, and that 'man's chief end is to glorify God, and to enjoy him for ever'.[2]

3:9 *God called to Adam … 'Where are you?'* This is the second question recorded in Genesis. God knew where they were, but He asked the question in order that they might acknowledge their sin. God calls the same question down the centuries to all mankind: 'Where are you?' The very fact that God searches us out shows His character. He acts first even though He is the one who has been sinned against. Supremely we see this in His providing the means of redemption and making moves towards us. Romans 5:8 says, 'While we were still sinners, Christ died for us.' We therefore see here a perfect example of how we ourselves should act when we have been sinned against. Love does not immediately withdraw communication when sinned against by a friend.

3:10 *I heard Your voice … and I was afraid.* The voice of God brings fear to the sinner. This is an important first stage in dealing with sin. There is hope when men and women have a fear of God. Many do not hear the voice of God at all, and heed no warning of impending judgement. Notice that Adam admits he hid himself and that he did this because he was aware of his nakedness.

3:11 *Have you eaten from the tree?* The question was asked by God, not because He did not know the answer, but again in order that Adam and Eve might admit their guilt. There can be no restitution without confession. We must walk in the light (1 John 1:7) and confess our sins (1 John 1:9).

3:12 *The woman whom You gave to be with me.* In reply to God's question 'Have you eaten of the tree?' Adam admits that he has done so, but blames Eve ('The woman … she gave me of the tree') and by implication also blames God ('The woman whom *You* gave', emphasis added). This is grievous indeed as Adam does not take full responsibility for his own sin. By blaming Eve and God he is hating her and God, which is akin to murder (Matt. 5:21–22; 15:19). Adam's Fall was deep and catastrophic.

3:13 *What is this you have done?* Eve again admits the sin of eating the fruit but blames the serpent and his deception. We notice that God does not ask the serpent 'What have you done?' There is no redemption for the devil and his angels, and no bringing to repentance.

---

14 So the Lord God said to the serpent: 'Because you have done this, you are cursed more than all cattle, and more than every beast of the field; on your belly you shall go, and you shall eat dust all the days of your life.

15 And I will put enmity between you and the woman, and between your seed and her Seed; He shall bruise your head, and you shall bruise His heel.'

16 To the woman He said: 'I will greatly multiply your sorrow and your conception; in pain you shall bring forth children; your desire shall be for your husband, and he shall rule over you.'

17 Then to Adam He said, 'Because you have heeded the voice of your wife, and have eaten from the tree of which I commanded you, saying, "You shall not eat of it": Cursed is the ground for your sake; in toil you shall eat of it all the days of your life.

18 Both thorns and thistles it shall bring forth for you, and you shall eat the herb of the field.

19 In the sweat of your face you shall eat bread till you return to the ground, for out of it you were taken; for dust you are, and to dust you shall return.'

20 And Adam called his wife's

name Eve, because she was the mother of all living.

21 Also for Adam and his wife the LORD God made tunics of skin, and clothed them.

22 Then the LORD God said, 'Behold, the man has become like one of Us, to know good and evil. And now, lest he put out his hand and take also of the tree of life, and eat, and live forever'—

23 therefore the LORD God sent him out of the garden of Eden to till the ground from which he was taken.

24 So He drove out the man; and He placed cherubim at the east of the garden of Eden, and a flaming sword which turned every way, to guard the way to the tree of life.

3:14 *You are cursed more than all cattle … On your belly you shall go.* The serpent is cursed and is brought to the ground, implying that it was possibly able to walk before. Certainly now the serpent would be in close contact with the ground which the Lord was about to curse.

3:14 *You shall eat dust all the days of your life.* Snakes constantly lick the dust. They have an organ in the roof of their mouths called the 'Jacobson's organ'. This enables the snake to smell by using its tongue. Using its forked tongue the snake constantly samples bits of dust. Once the tongue is pulled in, it inserts the tips of its forked tongue into the two openings of the Jacobson's organ, where the particles are identified and analysed.[3]

3:15 *Her Seed … He shall bruise your head and you shall bruise His heel.* This amazing statement right at the beginning, and immediately after the catastrophe of the Fall, is the foundation of all the promises of the Redeemer to come to rescue man. The woman would have a Seed: the virgin birth four thousand years later. This was in mind when Abraham looked by faith to the promise to come and it was counted to him for righteousness (15:6; 22:18; Gal. 3:16). Christ, the Seed of the woman, would bruise the serpent's head, but the serpent would nevertheless bruise His heel.

3:16 *I will greatly multiply your sorrow and your conception.* Human childbirth is harder than the bearing of young in the animal kingdom. Until the application of modern medical procedures, many women died in childbirth. Though mammals in the animal kingdom can also die when bearing their young, there is generally greater pain, difficulty and danger in human childbirth. Breach babies or babies across the womb used to pose a great danger to a woman's life; today, techniques including Caesarean operations are routinely performed to save both mother and child. Every birth is a reminder of what happened at the beginning.

3:16 *Your desire shall be for your husband.* Whereas before the Fall there was always mutual respect, which meant that Eve naturally could follow Adam's lead, now her desire is (subject to) her husband. A collision of wills is now bound to take place and Adam is to 'rule over' her.

3:17 *Cursed is the ground for your sake.* Adam was to know difficulty in providing for his wife and family. The ground which previously grew produce with little difficulty was now cursed, and thorns and thistles would throttle plants grown for food. 'In the sweat of your face you shall eat bread' (v. 19). Sweat speaks of the toil due to the curse, supremely seen on the Saviour's brow shortly after He had grappled with the awesome task of carrying our sin in the garden of Gethsemane (Luke 22:39–44). Man cannot take it easy. It will be hard and difficult for him to get his bread to provide for himself and his family. Note that man himself is *not* cursed. This is in contrast to the serpent, who is cursed.

3:18 *Both thorns and thistles it shall bring forth for you.* The ground will be significantly altered. The prevalence of unwanted growth and vegetation that were not part of the original good world emphasizes the effect of man's rebellion on the world and indeed on the whole creation. There is an allusion to the curse in Romans 8:21–22: 'the creature itself also will be delivered from the bondage of corruption into the glorious liberty of the children of God. For we know that the whole creation groans and labors with birth pangs together until now.' The creation groans under the curse.

There is evidence that thorns are formed from altered or modified leaves. It is an important issue that thorns are found fossilized in rock supposedly 300 million years old. (These dates are not correct; the rock is in fact flood rock which has buried the thorns.[4]) However, the Bible-believing Christian knows from Genesis 3 that thorns did not exist beforehand, and that the presence of thorns presupposes man's existence. This then immediately shows that creatures like dinosaurs, whose fossils are found higher up, were indeed in existence with man and the animals.

Significantly, thorns would be upon the brow of the Saviour as He took the curse for our sin upon Himself (Matt. 27:29). The day will come when the curse will finally be rolled back (Isa. 11:6–9).

3:19 *In the sweat of your face you shall eat bread*. Whereas beforehand the work that Adam did was easy and light, henceforward life would be very difficult and he would be constantly reminded that the ground he was tilling was cursed. His livelihood would now depend on his success. Adam is told he will return to dust. This is the penalty for sin. Adam had already experienced spiritual death (separation); now he and Eve would face physical death (separation of body and spirit).

This is the first mention of the word 'sweat', from the Hebrew *zeah*, which describes the effect of violent motion. It is connected to the word translated 'sweat' in Ezekiel 44:18, where the priests are told that 'they shall not clothe themselves with anything that causes sweat'. It is significant that the Saviour sweated heavily in the garden of Gethsemane (Luke 22:44), such that 'His sweat became like great drops of blood falling down to the ground'—the very ground that the Lord cursed in Genesis 3:17. The imagery and symbolism are powerful both in Genesis and in the Gospels, as having in sweat touched the cursed ground, He then shortly takes the crown of thorns, the symbol of our curse for sin.

3:19 *For dust you are, and to dust you shall return*. This shows that Adam was made literally from dust and *not* from pre-existing living material. It is a sad fact that when we die, our bodies rot and decay, and go to dust. God is therefore confirming in this sentence that Adam was made literally from dust. There was no pre-existing pre-Adamic race. Adam was made unique and different from all the other animals. He did not appear as *Homo divinus* after a long line of evolutionary development. Even the great John Stott stumbled in not recognizing that this verse does indeed require Adam to have been formed literally from dust.[5]

3:20 *The mother of all living*. Adam names his wife Eve, literally, 'life'.

3:21 *The LORD God made tunics of skin*. This is the first recorded instance of an implied sacrifice, since to have coats made of animal skins it is probable that a goat or lamb was killed; God thus provides a sacrifice symbolic of the Lamb to come, the Lord Jesus Christ.

Whereas in Genesis 2:25 they were naked and not ashamed, Adam and Eve now know that they are naked and are ashamed before God (3:7). Clothing was essential, for lust and greed needed to be restrained. The reason for clothing is difficult to justify if we accept the tenets of evolution and deny the historicity of Genesis. The animals are essentially unclothed, so why shouldn't we be? The ultimate appeal can only be to Genesis 3. It is noteworthy that it is always of the enemy, the devil, to bring confusion and moral degradation by unclothing men and women. An example is the disaster of the worship at the golden calf in Exodus 32 (see particularly vv. 6 and 22).

3:22 *Lest he … take also of the tree of life … and live forever.* Man is denied the eating of the tree of life. Before the Fall, the tree of life would have kept him alive for ever. Now he is denied it. Lest evil men and women live a long time and cause extended vice and brutality, God disallows them access to the tree of life. Dictators and evil people in every generation, though powerful, are limited by death. Death comes now to all. Only through Christ, our Substitute and Saviour, the way, the truth and the life (John 14:6), can we receive back the eternal life we lost in Eden.

3:23–24 *So He drove out the man.* Adam now has to gain his bread outside Eden, and the cherubim with the flaming sword guard the way back to the tree of life. Only in Revelation 22:2, 14 does the tree of life reappear and become accessible again; it is used for the healing of the nations, with the curse finally removed (Rev. 22:3). Before the Flood, the cherubim and the sword would have been a constant and visible witness of what man had fallen from and of the need for repentance. At the Flood, all that early world was swept away, but the new world has never been without a witness of the prophets. That constant witness to us is now preserved in the Scriptures.

Notes

1 **Spiros Zodhiates,** *Hebrew–Greek Study Bible* (Chattanooga, TN: AMG Publishers, 1986), commentary on Gen. 3:1–7, p. 5.

2 **Westminster Shorter Catechism,** answer to question 1: 'What is the chief end of man?'

3 See this article about the Jacobson's organ and the curse on the snake: **Gary Vaterlaus,** 'Left in the Dust', Answers in Genesis, 6 April 2009, https://answersingenesis.org/contradictions-in-the-bible/left-in-the-dust/.

4 **Ken Ham,** *Answers Book 4* (Green Forest, AR: Master Books, 2013), p. 18; and see 'Genesis 3 and the Meaning of the Crown of Thorns', Genesis Apologetics, 4 April 2015, http://genesisapologetics.com/genesis-3-and-the-meaning-of-the-crown-of-thorns/.

5 'But my acceptance of Adam and Eve as historical is not incompatible with my belief that several forms of pre-Adamic "hominid" may have existed for thousands of years previously. These hominids began to advance culturally. They made their cave drawings and buried their dead. It is conceivable that God created Adam out of one of them. You may call them *Homo erectus*. I think you may even call some of them *Homo sapiens*, for these are arbitrary scientific names. But Adam was the first *Homo divinus*, if I may coin a phrase, the first man to whom may be given the Biblical designation "made in the image of God"' (**John R. W. Stott,** *Understanding the Bible: Special Edition* (Milton Keynes: Scripture Union, 2011), p. 43.

Chapter 4

1 Now Adam knew Eve his wife, and she conceived and bore Cain, and said, 'I have acquired a man from the LORD.'

2 Then she bore again, this time his brother Abel. Now Abel was a keeper of sheep, but Cain was a tiller of the ground.

3 And in the process of time it came to pass that Cain brought an offering of the fruit of the ground to the LORD.

4 Abel also brought of the firstborn of his flock and of their fat. And the LORD respected Abel and his offering,

5 but He did not respect Cain and his offering. And Cain was very angry, and his countenance fell.

6 So the LORD said to Cain, 'Why are you angry? And why has your countenance fallen?

7 If you do well, will you not be accepted? And if you do not do well, sin lies at the door. And its desire is for you, but you should rule over it.'

4:1 *I have acquired a man from the LORD.* The first birth is recorded. The literal rendering in the Hebrew is 'I have got a man of the LORD' or 'I have got a man with the LORD'. Gill interprets Eve's saying as referring (mistakenly) to the promised Seed of Genesis 3:15, which no doubt she longed for to reverse the effects of the Fall. But she in fact gives birth to Cain, who refuses to walk in God's way and is hostile to God. Calvin allows this interpretation as a possibility, though favouring a simple giving of thanks for the first son born into the world. However, Eve calls this firstborn 'Cain', a name which comes from the Hebrew root word *qana*, meaning 'possession', 'inheritance'. The *Theological Wordbook of the Old Testament* and Gesenius' *Lexicon* show there is also a connection with the word *qayin*, 'spear' (see 2 Sam. 21:16).[1] The naming of her first son does then suggest that she did indeed think she had already obtained the answer to the serpent's deceit. Sadly, Cain proves to be the opposite.

4:2 *Then she bore again, this time his brother Abel.* The order of birth is first Cain (meaning 'possession') and then godly Abel ('breath'). This illustrates a principle which is mentioned in 1 Corinthians 15:47: 'The first man was of the earth, made of dust; the second Man is the Lord from heaven.' There are a number of other examples in Scripture where the spiritual succeeds the carnal: Ishmael/Isaac, Esau/Jacob and Saul/David. Abel was a keeper of sheep and Cain a tiller of the ground. Both occupations are, of themselves, honourable, but the symbolism is stark as Abel offers from the flock and Cain offers from the ground. Abel, like Jacob and David, understood blood sacrifice, but Cain, like Esau, did not.

4:3 *Cain brought an offering of the fruit of the ground.* Cain brought of the fruit of the ground, which God had cursed.

4:4 *Abel ... brought of the firstborn of his flock.* Abel brought a blood sacrifice which we read the Lord respected. This shows, firstly, that God requires a blood sacrifice, which is implied by the earlier covering of Adam and Eve in 3:21; and, secondly, that Adam had taught both brothers that this was required.

4:5 *Cain was very angry.* Note that the Scripture specifically gives the cause of Cain's anger: he was angry because his offering was not accepted and his anger was expressed against God directly. The Hebrew word for 'very' (*meod*) has great force and the word for 'angry' (*charah*) is translated in Exodus 22:24 and 32:10 as 'wrath [becoming/burning] hot'. The phrase 'blaze up in anger' would best describe Cain's reaction. 'Why was my offering refused?' is the essence of his furious outburst. So why was Cain's offering refused? Though there are instructions later concerning grain offerings (Lev. 2:1–16; 6:14–18; 7:9–10; 10:12–13), careful study reveals that because it was not a blood sacrifice it could not be used for atonement (Heb. 9:22) and was often used as an adjunct to the blood sacrifice of an animal (Exod. 29:38–46; Lev. 23:9–14; Num. 6:13–17; 7:13, 19, etc.; 8:8; 15:1–9). The grain offering was specifically *to follow the burnt offering* (Num. 28:5, 9, 12, 20, 26, 28; see also Josh. 22:23, 29; Judg. 13:19, 23). Cain brought to God what he himself thought was best. He had pride, rebellion and self-righteousness, and effectively, by bringing 'his best', he brought his self-righteousness as an offering to God. But he had forgotten that the ground was cursed and thus he ignored that he was a sinner by bringing a bloodless sacrifice before God's holiness. Cain had not offered a blood atonement, only a grain offering. This is the reason for God's refusal.

4:6 *Why are you angry?* As the Lord dealt with Adam and Eve in Genesis 3 when they sinned, so He deals with Cain: with a question. He confronts him with his sin.

4:7 *Sin lies at the door.* Most commentators take this to be a warning concerning sin itself crouching at the door: sin is likened to a predatory animal ready to pounce on the one who has a hostile attitude to the Lord.[2] However, other views were expressed by commentators from earlier centuries. John Gill (1697–1771) writes that this could be referring to the judgement of sin that is in danger of imminently coming upon Cain.[3] Gill and the Puritan Poole[4] also acknowledge another, more profound possibility which Adam Clarke's commentary on this passage brings out.[5] The Hebrew word *chattaath* for sin is the same as that used for 'sin offering' (Lev. 4:3, 8, 20–21, 24–25, 29, 32). Young's literal translation renders the word in Genesis 4:7 as 'sin offering'.[6] This translation brings out a deeper truth and highlights the grace of God as He deals with Cain. Under this interpretation, Cain has a vital choice. Does he let his anger grow further to murder, or does he even now take advantage of the sin offering that is available to him? God appeals to him to bring the sin offering so that he will be accepted.

4:7 *And its ['his', KJV] desire is for you, but you should rule over it ['him', KJV].* Gill and Clarke agree that this sentence is referring to Cain's birthright. Calvin also discusses this statement in the context of elder and younger brothers. In the light of the sin offering that is still available to him, Cain has no reason to be angry with Abel, or envious of him. Though Abel's offering has been accepted by God, Abel would still be subject to Cain, his elder brother; he would love Cain ('his desire is for you'), and Cain would still rule over him in civil affairs. Though we cannot be dogmatic on this interpretation, this does seem a more likely understanding of this passage as it avoids the unusual notion that we can rule over sin ('rule over it'), which is never alluded to elsewhere in Scripture. The reverse is alluded to (Rom. 6:14 says, 'For sin shall not have dominion over you'), but if sin's power is broken, it is never said that we rule over it.

8 Now Cain talked with Abel his brother; and it came to pass, when they were in the field, that Cain rose up against Abel his brother and killed him.

9 Then the LORD said to Cain, 'Where is Abel your brother?' He said, 'I do not know. Am I my brother's keeper?'

10 And He said, 'What have you done? The voice of your brother's blood cries out to Me from the ground.

11 So now you are cursed from the earth, which has opened its mouth to receive your brother's blood from your hand.

12 When you till the ground, it shall no longer yield its strength to you. A fugitive and a vagabond you shall be on the earth.'

13 And Cain said to the LORD, 'My punishment is greater than I can bear!

14 Surely You have driven me out this day from the face of the ground; I shall be hidden from Your face; I shall be a fugitive and a vagabond on the earth, and it will happen that anyone who finds me will kill me.'

15 And the LORD said to him, 'Therefore, whoever kills Cain, vengeance shall be taken on him sevenfold.' And the LORD set a mark on Cain, lest anyone finding him should kill him.

16 Then Cain went out from the presence of the LORD and dwelt in the land of Nod on the east of Eden.

4:8 *Cain rose up against Abel ... and killed him.* Cain refused the grace God had offered freely to him. Sin now takes its course and brings forth death ('sin, when it is full-grown, brings forth death', James 1:15).

4:9 *Where is Abel your brother?* It is striking that yet again God deals with sin by asking a question. And like the first question of God to Adam ('Where are you?', 3:9), this question, 'Where is your brother?', echoes down the generations to us. As Joseph said later to his brothers, 'You shall not see my face unless your brother is with you' (43:5); and the Lord made plain that we cannot expect the forgiveness of God if we do not love our brother: 'First be reconciled to your brother, and then come and offer your gift' (Matt. 5:24). In 1 John 4:20 we read, 'he who does not love his brother whom he has seen, how can he love God whom he has not seen?'

4:9 *Am I my brother's keeper?* We might have expected this famous retort from Cain to have invoked God's immediate judgement in the death penalty, but such is the grace of God that He still allows him to live, though with a mark upon him.

4:10 *The voice of your brother's blood cries out to Me from the ground.* The Lord Jesus Himself spoke of Abel's blood in Matthew 23:35: '… that on you may come all the righteous blood shed on the earth, from the blood of righteous Abel to the blood of Zechariah.' God does not forget the deaths of the innocent. This is a very sobering truth when we consider the number of children aborted today (in 2013 approx. 570 per day in the UK, over 3,000 per day in the US and over 115,000 per day worldwide). Only a tiny percentage will have been aborted because of a real risk to the survival of the mother.

4:11–12 *Cursed from the earth.* The Lord is here constantly alluding to the earth that was cursed at the first sin. The earth has absorbed Abel's blood. It would eventually receive the blood of the pure Lamb of God, who took the curse of sin in our place. Cain was cursed from the earth and would now not be able to get his food by tilling the ground. It is as though he had 'sown' the blood of his own brother in the earth and can now sow nothing else. He now becomes a fugitive and a wanderer. There is a sense of desperation and constant lament in the words 'fugitive' (Heb. *nuwa*, 'quiver', 'vacillate', 'tremble') and 'vagabond' (Heb. *nuwd*, 'one who 'laments', 'bemoans', 'shakes'). Jude 1:11 refers to the 'way of Cain': the human race is split into two families—the family of the saved and the family of the unsaved.

4:13–15 *My punishment is greater than I can bear!* The grace of God is such that God still responds to Cain's cries. Cain is concerned that he will be killed in revenge. In answer, the Lord sets a mark upon him so that no one will be able to take the life of Cain without incurring severe punishment. We don't know what this mark was, but it shows that God takes vengeance seriously. Deuteronomy 32:35 says, 'Vengeance is Mine'; and Paul quotes this in Romans 12:19: '"Vengeance is Mine, I will repay," says the Lord.'

4:16 *Cain went out from the presence of the* LORD. Such is the fate of the one who refuses the grace of God. We are reminded of Judas, who had had his feet washed by Christ at the Last Supper and yet still departed from the Lord. John 13:30 says, 'Having received the piece of bread, [Judas] then went out immediately. *And it was night*'; Acts 1:25 says, 'Judas by transgression fell, that he might go *to his own place*' (all emphasis added).

4:16 *Dwelt in the land of Nod.* Cain went into the land of Nod (lit. 'Wandering' in Hebrew).

---

17 And Cain knew his wife, and she conceived and bore Enoch. And he built a city, and called the name of the city after the name of his son—Enoch.

18 To Enoch was born Irad; and Irad begot Mehujael, and Mehujael begot Methushael, and Methushael begot Lamech.

19 Then Lamech took for himself two wives: the name of one was Adah, and the name of the second was Zillah.

20 And Adah bore Jabal. He was the father of those who dwell in tents and have livestock.

21 His brother's name was Jubal. He was the father of all those who play the harp and flute.

22 And as for Zillah, she also bore Tubal-Cain, an instructor of every craftsman in bronze and iron. And the sister of Tubal-Cain was Naamah.

23 Then Lamech said to his wives: 'Adah and Zillah, hear my voice; wives of Lamech, listen to my speech! For I have killed a man for wounding me, even a young man for hurting me.

24 If Cain shall be avenged sevenfold, then Lamech seventy-sevenfold.'

25 And Adam knew his wife again, and she bore a son and named him Seth, 'For God has appointed another seed for me instead of Abel, whom Cain killed.'

26 And as for Seth, to him also a son was born; and he named him Enosh. Then men began to call on the name of the LORD.

4:17 *Cain knew his wife, and she … bore Enoch.* We are not told who Cain's wife was, but Genesis 5:4 does tell us that Adam 'had sons and daughters', so evidently Cain married his sister (or possibly his niece). According to Josephus, Jewish tradition held that the number of children in total born to Adam and Eve was thirty-three sons and twenty-three daughters.[7] At this point at the beginning of the human race the danger of degenerative mutations causing genetic deformations and diseases was slight,[8] which is why it was not until approximately 2,500 years later that laws against incest were introduced by Moses in Leviticus 18–20. Note that the text does not say Cain found a wife in the land of Nod, as though some extra-Adamic people were there. He would have taken one of his sisters as wife before he arrived there.

Cain builds a city and calls it after his son. Significantly, the first city is in Cain's line. The concentration of evil later at Babel is dispersed by God (Gen. 11).

4:18 *Enoch … Irad … Mehujael … Methushael … Lamech.* Enoch means 'initiator', Irad means 'fleet as a wild ass', Mehujael means 'smitten of God', Methushael means 'who is of God' and Lamech means 'powerful'. Barnes comments on Genesis 4:18 that 'we … find a value put upon youth and physical superiority, as the fleetness of the wild ass'.[9] As Matthew Henry states, Cain's line shows that Cain 'cast off all pretensions to the fear of God, and never … attended on God's ordinances any more'.[10]

4:19 *Lamech took for himself two wives … Adah … Zillah.* The first mention of polygamy, which shows Cain's departure from God's pathway. Adah means 'ornament', 'beauty', and Zillah means 'shade'.

4:20–22 *Adah bore Jabal … Jubal.* There is no mention of calling upon God, as in Seth's line (4:26); rather there is cattle husbandry (Adah's son Jabal), music (Adah's other son, Jubal), industry and commerce (Zillah's son Tubal-Cain). This also shows that knowledge of industry, including metal working (v. 22), was well advanced, so that the later massive undertaking of building the ark in the time of Noah was perfectly feasible.

4:23–24 *Lamech said … I have killed a man for wounding me, even a young man for hurting me.* Most commentators think that Lamech is bragging rather than demonstrating any sense of remorse. Some suggest that two murders were involved, requiring the use of weapons made by his son Tubal-Cain. There is a sense of proud and presumptuous self-confidence in his boasting to his wives, who naturally would have been deeply concerned about the ongoing danger of revenge and further bloodshed.

4:25 … *Named him Seth. 'For God has appointed another seed for me instead of Abel.'* Seth means 'appointed' or 'compensation', and headed the godly line.

4:26 *Then men began to call on the name of the* LORD. After such a downward spiral of sin and sadness, this sentence is deliberately placed to show that God always has a remnant who love Him. The name Enosh means 'mortal' or 'frail' and indicates that Seth understood man's real fallen condition. Seth's offspring now call upon the name of the Lord. Most commentators regard this as a serious invoking and use of the name of God, both in the establishing of a dynasty which would be separate from Cain's line, and in praying together to God.

Notes

1 **R. Laird Harris, Gleason L. Archer Jr. and Bruce K. Waltke,** *Theological Wordbook of the Old Testament,* vol. 2 (Chicago: Moody, 1980), pp. 797–798; and **Willhelm Gesenius,** *Hebrew and Chaldee Lexicon to the Old Testament Scriptures,* tr. Samuel Prideaux Tregelles (London: Samuel Bagster and Sons, 1857), p. 731.

2 For example, **Eveson,** *Book of Origins.*

3 **John Gill,** *Exposition of the Old and New Testament,* 1746–1763.

4 **Matthew Poole,** *Commentary on the Whole Bible.*

5 **Adam Clarke,** *Commentary on the Whole Bible,* 1810–1826.

6 **Robert Young,** *Literal Translation of the Holy Bible: Revised* (Edinburgh, 1898).

7 **F. Josephus,** *The Complete Works of Josephus* (Grand Rapids: Kregel, 1981), p. 27.

8 **Ken Ham (ed.),** *Answers Book 1* (Green Forest, AR: Master Books, 2006), pp. 71–72.

9 **Albert Barnes,** *Notes on the Whole Bible,* 1834.

10 **Henry,** *Commentary,* Gen. 4:16–18.

Chapter 5

1 This is the book of the genealogy of Adam. In the day that God created man, He made him in the likeness of God.

2 He created them male and female, and blessed them and called them Mankind in the day they were created.

3 And Adam lived one hundred and thirty years, and begot a son in his own likeness, after his image, and named him Seth.

4 After he begot Seth, the days of Adam were eight hundred years; and he had sons and daughters.

5 So all the days that Adam lived were nine hundred and thirty years; and he died.

6 Seth lived one hundred and five years, and begot Enosh.

7 After he begot Enosh, Seth lived eight hundred and seven years, and had sons and daughters.

8 So all the days of Seth were nine hundred and twelve years; and he died.

9 Enosh lived ninety years, and begot Cainan.

10 After he begot Cainan, Enosh lived eight hundred and fifteen years, and had sons and daughters.

11 So all the days of Enosh were nine hundred and five years; and he died.

12 Cainan lived seventy years, and begot Mahalalel.

13 After he begot Mahalalel, Cainan lived eight hundred and forty years, and had sons and daughters.

14 So all the days of Cainan were nine hundred and ten years; and he died.

15 Mahalalel lived sixty-five years, and begot Jared.

16 After he begot Jared, Mahalalel lived eight hundred and thirty years, and had sons and daughters.

17 So all the days of Mahalalel were eight hundred and ninety-five years; and he died.

18 Jared lived one hundred and sixty-two years, and begot Enoch.

19 After he begot Enoch, Jared lived eight hundred years, and had sons and daughters.

20 So all the days of Jared were nine hundred and sixty-two years; and he died.

21 Enoch lived sixty-five years, and begot Methuselah.

22 After he begot Methuselah, Enoch walked with God three

hundred years, and had sons and daughters.

23 So all the days of Enoch were three hundred and sixty-five years.

24 And Enoch walked with God; and he was not, for God took him.

25 Methuselah lived one hundred and eighty-seven years, and begot Lamech.

26 After he begot Lamech, Methuselah lived seven hundred and eighty-two years, and had sons and daughters.

27 So all the days of Methuselah were nine hundred and sixty-nine years; and he died.

28 Lamech lived one hundred and eighty-two years, and had a son.

29 And he called his name Noah, saying, 'This one will comfort us concerning our work and the toil of our hands, because of the ground which the LORD has cursed.'

30 After he begot Noah, Lamech lived five hundred and ninety-five years, and had sons and daughters.

31 So all the days of Lamech were seven hundred and seventy-seven years; and he died.

32 And Noah was five hundred years old, and Noah begot Shem, Ham, and Japheth.

5:5 *So all the days that Adam lived were nine hundred and thirty years; and he died.* This chapter in Genesis is most instructive when taken as a whole. Firstly, it shows the obvious point that all Adam's descendants must now die: 'in Adam all die' (1 Cor. 15:22). Secondly, by using charts such as those in *Genesis for Today* it is possible to see who was alive at which period, and, in particular, how many generations could have been alive at any one time. We know from Jude 14 that the names are correct in Genesis 5 (with no omissions), since the words 'Enoch the seventh from Adam' confirm the list of Genesis 5. Also, we note that the names are listed again in 1 Chronicles 1 and Luke 3. The possibilities of direct communication back to Adam are striking. Incredible as it seems in our time, which is so far removed from the time of Genesis, Adam was still alive when his descendant *eight generations after him* (Lamech) was a man of thirty! There were roughly one thousand years from the creation of Adam to the birth of Noah, and according to Genesis 11 there were roughly one thousand years from the birth of Noah to the birth of Abraham.

Thirdly, there seems an intention in the names. There are ten names from Adam down to and including Noah: Adam—Seth—Enosh—Cainan—Mahalalel—Jared—Enoch—Methuselah—Lamech—Noah. There is a hint of the gospel in the meanings of these names. The first four names (Adam—Seth—Enosh—Cainan) mean Man—Appointed—Mortal—Sorrow. Mahalalel means 'the God who is to be praised', and Jared means 'descent' or 'coming down', so that couplet speaks of God eventually coming down to man. The last four names (Enoch—Methuselah—Lamech—Noah) mean, in order: Teaching—His death shall bring—Despairing—Rest, which some suggest may be a veiled reference to Christ and His death for His people.

5:21 *Enoch lived sixty-five years, and begot Methuselah.* Godly Enoch called his son's name Methuselah, which means 'when he is dead it will come' or 'his death will bring'. Remarkably, Enoch knew that the Flood would come nigh on a thousand years before it happened. Jude shows the godliness of Enoch, who foresaw the Second Coming of Christ, saying, 'the Lord comes with ten thousands of His saints' (Jude 14).

5:22 *After he begot Methuselah, Enoch walked with God.* Unlike all the others in this list of descendants, of whom it is said that they simply 'lived' after they begot a named son, here it specifically says that Enoch 'walked with God' after begetting Methuselah.

5:24 *Enoch walked with God.* Such was Enoch's walk with God that God took him. Hebrews 11:5 shows that he was translated to heaven without death, the only other person to experience this being Elijah. Hebrews 11:5 states that 'before he was taken he had this testimony, that he pleased God'. The beginning of that verse says, 'By faith Enoch was taken away so that he did not see death'—thus showing that very early on it was always salvation by grace through faith which enabled men and women, though fallen, to walk with God.

5:29 *He [Lamech] called his name Noah, saying, 'This one will comfort us.'* The birth of Noah, whose name means 'Rest' or 'Comfort'. He is a type of Christ, since in his day he builds the place of rescue from the impending judgement. Lamech died five years before his father Methuselah and overlapped Adam by fifty-six years. Consequently, at this time, much would have been known accurately concerning the beginning of the ante-diluvian world. Noah overlapped Methuselah for 600 years and Methuselah overlapped Adam's latter 243 years. There is no doubt godly Enoch would have talked with Adam, whom he knew for 308 years, and would also have instructed Methuselah, Lamech and Noah. Noah would carry the truth of creation primarily from Methuselah, his grandfather, who very likely had known and talked with Adam.

5:32 *And Noah was five hundred years old, and Noah begot Shem, Ham, and Japheth.* Through comparing 5:32 with 9:22, 24 (Ham is referred to as Noah's 'younger son'), 10:21 (Japheth is referred to as 'the elder') and 11:10 (Shem is one hundred years old two years after the Flood) we can deduce the likely age order of the children. However, the argument is not conclusive, since 9:24 may be a reference to Canaan— see commentary for that verse below. Because the Flood occurred when Noah was 600 years old (7:6), this implies that Noah was 502 years old when Shem was born. For 5:32 to hold, Japheth was probably born when Noah was 500 years old, and it is probable that the actual chronological order of Noah's three children was Japheth, Shem and then Ham. Shem is mentioned first because he carries the greater blessing compared with this brothers. From him comes the godly line down to Abraham (Gen. 11). If this order of the sons of Noah is correct, then again we note that it is the second son who is the one who carries the blessing (as with Abel, Isaac and Jacob).

Chapter 6

1 Now it came to pass, when men began to multiply on the face of the earth, and daughters were born to them,

2 that the sons of God saw the daughters of men, that they were beautiful; and they took wives for themselves of all whom they chose.

3 And the LORD said, 'My Spirit shall not strive with man forever, for he is indeed flesh; yet his days shall be one hundred and twenty years.'

4 There were giants on the earth in those days, and also afterward, when the sons of God came in to the daughters of men and they bore children to them. Those were the mighty men who were of old, men of renown.

6:1 *When men began to multiply on the face of the earth.* The suggestion is that there was a large population in the world immediately prior to the Flood. It is difficult to know whether this was measured in millions or not. From Genesis 5 and 7:6 we know there were 1,656 years from the creation of Adam to the year of the Flood. Population programmes suggest millions, but much depends on the age when sons and offspring were born and the number of offspring per generation. The specific mention of multiplying in the context of the rise of evil (6:5) and the knowledge that the godly line tended to have children late (Gen. 5) suggests that the line of Cain may have been multiplying much faster than that of Seth. Nevertheless, that only Noah's family were found righteous suggests the entrance of disbelief, sinful thoughts and practices into Seth's descendants as well.

6:2 *The sons of God saw the daughters of men, that they were beautiful, and they took wives for themselves of all whom they chose.* An obvious—but important—lesson is that it was the sons of God who did the choosing, and there is no mention of the Lord leading them. The context is the development of evil. For the first marriage, that of Adam to Eve, '[God] brought her to the man' (1:22), but here in 6:2 it is the outward physical attraction alone which is leading to ungodly unions.

6:2–4 *There were giants on the earth in those days … the sons of God came in to the daughters of men.* The offspring of these ungodly unions were giants. The Hebrew word is *nephilim*, which comes from the Hebrew verb *naphal*, which means 'to fall' and is often translated 'to overthrow, fall upon'. These giants were thus associated with violence and rebellion.

Who were the sons of God? There are two main views. Some (notably John Gill) say that this refers to the godly line of Seth intermarrying with the line of Cain—though we do not know from the text that all the line of Cain were ungodly. Others (notably Henry Morris, *Defender's Study Bible*, and John MacArthur, *MacArthur Study Bible*) think this is referring to fallen angels. This view is not without warrant, given that the phrase 'sons of God' is elsewhere always used of angels (Job 1:6; 2:1; 38:7); that the Hebrew construction translated 'mighty ones' or 'children of God' (Ps. 29:1; 82:6; 89:6) again usually refers to heavenly beings; and that 2 Peter 2:4 and Jude 6 refer to angels who sinned, with explicit reference to their leaving 'their proper domain' (Jude 6), and this in the context of sexual sin (Jude 7). Matthew 22:30 (no marriage in heaven) is not a strong counter-argument nor conclusive, since the issue at hand is not the angels of God, but the sin of evil angels.[1] It is advisable not to be dogmatic and to concentrate on what we do know for certain; namely, that there was untempered sexual activity and that evil was rampant, so much so that only one family in the whole world was godly.

6:3 *His days shall be one hundred and twenty years.* From this we deduce that the warning to Noah came 120 years before the Flood, which began in the six hundredth year of Noah's life (7:6); thus the warning was given when Noah was approximately 480 years old. In 5:32 we learn that Noah was 500 years old, so that as God spoke to him in Genesis 6 and gave him the order to make an ark, he must have been at least 500 years old. Thus it is inferred that Noah took about a hundred years to build the ark, during which time the Lord is described as being longsuffering and patient (1 Peter 3:20), while Noah preached righteousness to a lost world who would not listen (2 Peter 2:5).

5 Then the Lord saw that the wickedness of man was great in the earth, and that every intent of the thoughts of his heart was only evil continually.

6 And the Lord was sorry that He had made man on the earth, and He was grieved in His heart.

7 So the Lord said, 'I will destroy man whom I have created from the face of the earth, both man and beast, creeping thing and birds of the air, for I am sorry that I have made them.'

8 But Noah found grace in the eyes of the Lord.

9 This is the genealogy of Noah. Noah was a just man, perfect in his generations. Noah walked with God.

10 And Noah begot three sons: Shem, Ham, and Japheth.

11 The earth also was corrupt before God, and the earth was filled with violence.

12 So God looked upon the earth, and indeed it was corrupt; for all flesh had corrupted their way on the earth.

13 And God said to Noah, 'The end of all flesh has come before Me, for the earth is filled with violence through them; and behold, I will destroy them with the earth.'

6:5 *Then the Lord saw ... the wickedness of man.* There is nothing that God does not see. There is a vital lesson here in how each one of us should live. None can escape the eye of God.

6:5 *Every intent of the thoughts of his heart was only evil continually.* By nature we are all children of wrath (Eph. 2:3). The heart of man left to itself is corrupt (Jer. 17:9–10; Rom. 1:21).

6:6 *And the Lord was sorry ... He was grieved in His heart*. The King James Version translates the first phrase 'And it repented the Lord', with the word translated 'repented' being the Hebrew word *nacham*, which has an onomatopoeic connection to drawing the breath forcibly. It is sometimes translated 'pant' or 'groan'. It graphically describes the Lord's anguish over the evil of men. The phrase 'grieved in His heart' and the description of man's heart in the preceding verse are the first mentions of 'heart' in Scripture (from

Heb. *leb*, meaning the deepest seat of one's emotions and decisions). This shows that the Lord is deeply concerned about the evil in man's heart, and that His Spirit is intertwined in human affairs.

6:7 *I will destroy man whom I have created.* The word translated 'destroy' is very strong. The Hebrew is *machah* and is used elsewhere in the Flood account (see 7:4, 23). It can be rendered 'blot out' or 'exterminate' and clearly has that sense here. It is translated 'utterly blot out' in Exodus 17:14 concerning Amalek, and 'blot out' in Exodus 32:32–33 and Deuteronomy 9:14 when Moses argues in prayer with the Lord concerning the sin of the people of Israel and the golden calf (see also the same word used in 2 Kings 21:13 concerning Jerusalem; in Ps. 51:1, 9 concerning the sin of David; and in Ps. 9:5; 69:28 concerning the final judgement of the wicked). Its use here in Genesis 6 reflects the furious judgement of God, and coupled with the description of the Lord's heart in 6:6 underlines that the Lord is *not* passive in the face of the world's rejection of Him. It is only because of the Lord's mercy that He has not yet judged the world today, but He sees all and will bring about the final separation of the righteous from the wicked (see the imagery of the separation of wheat from tares in Matt. 13:24–30 and the Lord's patience in not immediately rooting them out). This is very pertinent to our own world today, since the Lord Jesus Himself said that 'as it was in the days of Noah, so it will be also in the days of the Son of Man' (Luke 17:26).

6:8 *Noah found grace in the eyes of the LORD.* It is only because of the Lord's grace that anyone is saved, and Hebrews 11:7 emphasizes that Noah walked by faith, believing the warnings of God. The name of Noah's grandfather, Methuselah, would have been a constant reminder that judgement was coming (see notes above on 5:21), and God spoke directly to Noah (6:3, 13) of the judgement he was going to bring. Noah finding the grace of God is a graphic illustration of how sinners can receive such grace today (Eph. 2:4–8) with God's impending judgement looming.

6:9 *A just man, perfect.* 'Just' is from the Hebrew *tsaddiyq*, meaning 'righteous'; and 'perfect' is from *tamiym*, 'upright', 'complete'. Noah is a spiritually saved person, not because of his own righteousness but because of God's grace upon him. The word *tamiym* is used of the Passover lamb (Exod. 12:5, 'without blemish') and the root word, *tam*, is used of Job (Job 1:8). It is also used of Jacob in Genesis 25:27: although he is described as 'mild', the word *tam* is still here being used in the deeper sense of 'perfect', 'without blemish', indicating an imputed righteousness for Jacob as against his brother Esau, who had no such righteousness.

6:9 *Walked with God*. Only Enoch (5:22, 24) and Noah are described as walking with God. However, the imagery in 3:8 is similar to this, referring to the practice of Adam to commune regularly with God before the Fall. Likewise, Abraham is described as 'the friend of God' (James 2:23), Moses is the man whom God knows 'face to face' (Exod. 33:11; Num. 12:8; Deut. 34:10), and Daniel is the man 'greatly beloved' (Dan. 9:23; 10:11; 10:19).

6:11 *Corrupt before God ... filled with violence*. The corruption and violence flowed from the 'intent of the thoughts of [man's] heart' (see 6:5). 'For as he thinks in his heart, so is he' (Prov. 23:7); 'For out of the heart proceed evil thoughts, murders, adulteries, fornications, thefts, false witness, blasphemies' (Matt. 15:19). The Lord will judge such. 'It is a fearful thing to fall into the hands of the living God' (Heb. 10:31). A world defying God is a fearful thing but will be seen again in the days leading up to the coming judgement. The comparison with our present age is striking: 'Know this, that in the last days perilous times will come' (2 Tim. 3:1); 'scoffers will come in the last days, walking according to their own lusts, and saying, "Where is the promise of His coming?"' (2 Peter 3:3–4).

6:12 *All flesh*. The words here do include animal flesh, since exactly the same two words are used throughout the Flood account (see 6:13, 17, 19; 7:15–16, 21; 8:17; 9:11, 15–17). God is concerned not only about men and women, but also about animals. Though animals have no moral choice, the text does speak here of the fact that all flesh 'had corrupted their way' (Heb. *derek*, 'manner of life', 'habit'), which may refer to further sexual immorality involving bestiality, though this cannot be proved. The penalty commanded later for such immorality was death (Exod. 22:19; Lev. 20:15), for both the person and the animal concerned.

6:13 *I will destroy them with the earth*. A repeat of the essence of verse 7, but this time repeating the word 'corrupt' (here translated 'destroy'; Heb. *shaccath*, 'ruin', 'corrupt', 'spoil', 'destroy') of verse 12 ('corrupted their way') as part of the judgment: 'I will *ruin* them with the earth.' The repetition of God's judgement (6:7, 13, 17; 7:4) underlines the certainty that it is not going to be revoked.

6:13 *With the earth*. This phrase shows that the earth will be destroyed, and with 6:7 ('destroy … from the face of the earth') implies that the *whole earth* will suffer destruction. Similarly, 6:17 again emphasizes that everything on the land that has the 'breath of life' will die. The worldwide nature of the imminent Flood is paralleled by the worldwide nature of Christ's return still to come upon our world in Luke 17:26 and 2 Peter 3:3–6.

---

14 'Make yourself an ark of gopherwood; make rooms in the ark, and cover it inside and outside with pitch.

15 And this is how you shall make it: The length of the ark shall be three hundred cubits, its width fifty cubits, and its height thirty cubits.

16 You shall make a window for the ark, and you shall finish it to a cubit from above; and set the door of the ark in its side. You shall make it with lower, second, and third decks.

17 And behold, I Myself am bringing floodwaters on the earth, to destroy from under heaven all flesh in which is the breath of life; everything that is on the earth shall die.

18 But I will establish My covenant with you; and you shall go into the ark—you, your sons, your wife, and your sons' wives with you.

19 And of every living thing of all flesh you shall bring two of every sort into the ark, to keep them alive with you; they shall be male and female.

20 Of the birds after their kind, of animals after their kind, and of every creeping thing of the earth after its kind, two of every kind will come to you to keep them alive.

21 And you shall take for yourself of all food that is eaten, and you shall gather it to yourself; and it shall be food for you and for them.'

22 Thus Noah did; according to all that God commanded him, so he did.

6:14 *Make yourself an ark of gopherwood … Cover it inside and outside with pitch*. Noah is to 'make' the ark (Heb. *asah*, 'make', 'prepare'). The same word is used to describe God making man (1:26). Noah is to prepare the ark according to God's instructions using gopherwood. No one has been able conclusively to identify the wood used; some have suggested cypress or cedar—both trees are used for shipbuilding. The pitch might not have been a bituminous pitch as the word used here in the Hebrew is *kopher*, which is the same as *kaphar* and is translated later (e.g. Lev. 17:11) as 'atonement'.[2] Though we cannot be dogmatic, some have therefore suggested that it was blood-based in some way. As Morris comments in his *Defender's Study Bible*, 'in providing a protective covering against the waters of judgment, it thus becomes a beautiful type of Christ'.

6:15 *The length of the ark shall be three hundred cubits.* Caricatures of the ark in children's literature do great damage to this awesome and careful work of construction that took 120 years to complete. The ark was roughly 450 feet (137.1 metres) long, 75 feet (22.9 metres) wide and 45 feet (13.7 metres) tall. One military troopship of Greece built in 200 BC reached almost the size of the ark: the Tessarakonteres, which was 420 feet (120 metres) long. A vessel reaching beyond the dimensions of the ark was not made till the SS *Great Eastern* built in 1858 by Brunel and which was 680 feet (207 metres) by 83 feet (25.2) by 58 feet (9.1 metres). The ark was about twice the length of a Boeing 747, which is 232 feet long (70.7 metres). Many have tried to debunk the validity of these dimensions, supposing that the people of that time could not have had the knowledge to build such a large wooden ship, but they fail to see that there is evidence that earlier peoples were more advanced in some aspects of engineering than we are today. Some architecture dating to immediately after the Flood still baffles engineers today—for example, the pyramids at Giza in Egypt, with the immense inner blocks of the Great Pyramid precisely positioned such that they interlock; or the stone wall at Sacsayhuamán in Peru, whose stones of different sizes are positioned such that a razor blade cannot be put between them. It is proposed by sceptical marine archaeologists that ships beyond 300 feet in length could not have been built out of wood because of the hogging difficulty (in which a heaving sea will bend the wood longitudinally, so causing planks to separate as waves come underneath). However, the fact that the Greeks built the troopship Tessarakonteres out of wood, and close to the length of the ark, negates such scepticism and shows that such problems were countered by sophisticated methods of attaching the beams together (called 'planking' in marine archaeology). The method used was mortice and tenon-jointed planks, which goes back to at least the fourteenth century BC.[3] Tests have been done on the dimensions of the biblical ark which show beyond doubt that the ark was built for stability, being very difficult to capsize.[4]

6:16 *You shall make a window for the ark ... lower, second, and third decks.* The ark was specifically designed with three levels and a window opening of approximately 1.5 feet (0.5 metres) for air. Note that the ark described in the writings of the Mesopotamian *Epic of Gilgamesh* is a perfect cube with a side dimension of 200 feet (70 metres) and seven storeys high. Such a craft would roll on the open sea, and it is obvious to a nautical engineer that the account in Genesis is using sea-going proportions and that the Gilgamesh version is a fanciful corruption.

A further important point is that a clay tablet has been found in the ancient Babylonian city of Nippur which clearly *predates* the *Epic of Gilgamesh*. It dates from about 2200 BC, or soon after the Flood itself, and there is no detail on this tablet that differs from the detail in Genesis, with nothing extra added in. This earlier tablet thereby shows that the Genesis account is indeed the true account and is older than the Babylonian corrupted version.[5]

6:17 *I Myself am bringing floodwaters on the earth.* The word 'flood' here translates the first use of Hebrew *mabbul*, which is translated in the Septuagint as *kataklysmos*, from which we get 'cataclysmic'— underlining the huge significance of this event. The possible mechanisms of this worldwide event are discussed below at 7:11.

6:17 *Everything that is on the earth shall die.* This verse and 6:7; 7:4 are very clear that this is a worldwide event. One might well ask, if the Flood was a local flood as proposed by Hugh Ross and others,[6] what would have been the point of building a sophisticated boat if all one had to do was go to the nearest high mountain?

6:18 *I will establish My covenant with you.* As with Abraham later (17:2), God makes a covenant with Noah. God's grace is sealed in His covenant agreements.

6:19 *Of every living thing of all flesh you shall bring two of every sort into the ark ... male and female.* John Woodmorappe has shown that there was ample room in the ark for about 125,000 animals about the size of sheep.[7]

Even if we identify 'kind' with 'species' that is used in biology today (which is probably not the case as 'kinds' are more likely to be identified with the family grouping or possibly genus), this leads to estimates of the number of current species of land animals to be only somewhere around 18,000; if we then allow for known extinct species and seven (pairs) of the few clean kinds of animals, Noah would have needed no more than about 50,000 land animals in total on the ark, with the average size being less than that of a sheep. In fact, with 'kind' identified with 'family', these numbers would be considerably less. Consequently there was ample room on the ark for all the creatures. The food (6:21) and Noah's living quarters would take up the remainder.

6:20 *Two of every kind will come to you.* Notice that it is God who brings all the animals to Noah. God directed the animals to the ark, possibly increasing the awareness of impending danger that animals are known to have. Certainly the gathering of pairs of animals is God's work and Noah simply opens the ark to the animals coming in.

Note

1 See **T. Chaffey,** 'Who Are the "Sons of God"?', in *Answers* 7, no. 7 (2012), for a summary of the different views on this passage.

2 See **Harris, Archer and Waltke,** *Theological Wordbook of the Old Testament.*

3 See **Lionel Casson,** *The Ancient Mariners* (2nd ed.; Princeton, NJ: Princeton University Press, 1991), p. 108.

4 See **S. W. Hong et. al.,** 'Safety Investigation of Noah's Ark in a Seaway', in *Creation Technical Journal* 8, no. 1 (1994): 26–35; **D. H. Collins,** 'Was Noah's Ark Stable?', in *Creation Research Society Quarterly* 14 (1977): 83–87; **Ken Ham and Tim Lovett,** 'Was There Really a Noah's Ark and Flood?', Answers in Genesis, 15 February 2014, https://answersingenesis.org/the-flood/global/was-there-really-a-noahs-ark-flood/; and also the very thorough website of **Tim Lovett,** Noah's Ark: Impossible for Ancient People?, at http://worldwideflood.com/objections/ancients_incapable.htm.

5 See **John Morris,** 'Genesis, Gilgamesh, and an Early Flood Tablet', *Acts & Facts* 40, no. 11 (2011): 16. For a good comparison of other accounts of the Flood with the Genesis account, see pp. 2–3 of **Clive Anderson and Brian Edwards,** *Evidence for the Bible* (Leominster: Day One, 2014).

6 See, for instance, **Krista Bontrager,** 'Biblical Foundation for RTB's Flood Model', Reasons to Believe, 1 June 2011, http://www.reasons.org/articles/biblical-foundation-for-rtb's-flood-model.

7 **John Woodmorappe,** *Noah's Ark: A Feasibility Study* (El Cajon: Inst. for Creation Research, 1996).

Chapter 7

1 Then the LORD said to Noah, 'Come into the ark, you and all your household, because I have seen that you are righteous before Me in this generation.

2 You shall take with you seven each of every clean animal, a male and his female; two each of animals that are unclean, a male and his female;

3 also seven each of birds of the air, male and female, to keep the species alive on the face of all the earth.

4 For after seven more days I will cause it to rain on the earth forty days and forty nights, and I will destroy from the face of the earth all living things that I have made.'

5 And Noah did according to all that the LORD commanded him.

6 Noah was six hundred years old when the floodwaters were on the earth.

7 So Noah, with his sons, his wife, and his sons' wives, went into the ark because of the waters of the flood.

8 Of clean animals, of animals that are unclean, of birds, and of everything that creeps on the earth,

9 two by two they went into the ark to Noah, male and female, as God had commanded Noah.

7:1 *Come into the ark, you and all your household.* This invitation is echoed in Matthew 11:28: 'Come to Me, all you who labor and are heavy laden, and I will give you rest.' God invites men and women now to come 'into the ark'—that is, the gospel ark—and to be saved from the judgement which is surely coming upon us.

7:1 *I have seen that you are righteous.* There is a similarity to Job 1:1, where Job is described as righteous in his generation.

7:2 *You shall take with you seven of every clean animal.* Either this is seven pairs or three pairs with one left for sacrifice when Noah left the ark (8:20). But given 7:3—'also seven … male and female', most take this to mean seven pairs of clean animals.

7:4 *After seven more days.* The animals and Noah had come into the ark a week before the Flood began. The mocking and jeering of the unbelieving crowd would have been strong as the ark was being prepared—see 1 Peter 3:20: 'when once the Divine longsuffering waited in the days of Noah, while the ark was being prepared, in which a few, that is, eight souls, were saved'; and 2 Peter 2:5: 'but [God] saved Noah, one of eight people, a preacher of righteousness'. Now, after the many animals and the family had gone in (repeated for emphasis in 7:7), there was still time for repentance in that final week, with the door open and the way of escape from the impending doom still available.

7:4 *Forty days and forty nights.* This is the first mention of the number 'forty', which is often associated with the idea of testing and difficulty. Moses fasted forty days and nights (Exod. 24:18; 34:28; Deut. 9:11, 18, 25; 10:10), the children of Israel were forty years in the wilderness (Num. 14:33–34; 32:13), Goliath challenged the army of Israel for forty days (1 Sam. 17:16), Elijah fasted for forty days (1 Kings 19:8), and the Lord Himself fasted and was tempted for forty days (Luke 4:2).

7:5 *Noah did according to all that the LORD commanded him.* This was the secret to the blessing of the Lord upon him. Noah obeyed in a sore test of faith with no one, bar his own immediate family, going with him. Abraham did the same later—he left Ur, 'not knowing where he was going' (Heb. 11:8).

---

10 And it came to pass after seven days that the waters of the flood were on the earth.

11 In the six hundredth year of Noah's life, in the second month, the seventeenth day of the month, on that day all the fountains of the great deep were broken up, and the windows of heaven were opened.

12 And the rain was on the earth forty days and forty nights.

13 On the very same day Noah and Noah's sons, Shem, Ham, and Japheth, and Noah's wife and the three wives of his sons with them, entered the ark—

14 they and every beast after its kind, all cattle after their kind, every creeping thing that creeps on the earth after its kind, and every bird after its kind, every bird of every sort.

15 And they went into the ark to Noah, two by two, of all flesh in which is the breath of life.

16 So those that entered, male and female of all flesh, went in as God

had commanded him; and the LORD shut him in.

17 Now the flood was on the earth forty days. The waters increased and lifted up the ark, and it rose high above the earth.

18 The waters prevailed and greatly increased on the earth, and the ark moved about on the surface of the waters.

19 And the waters prevailed exceedingly on the earth, and all the high hills under the whole heaven were covered.

20 The waters prevailed fifteen cubits upward, and the mountains were covered.

21 And all flesh died that moved on the earth: birds and cattle and beasts and every creeping thing that creeps on the earth, and every man.

22 All in whose nostrils was the breath of the spirit of life, all that was on the dry land, died.

23 So He destroyed all living things which were on the face of the ground: both man and cattle, creeping thing and bird of the air. They were destroyed from the earth. Only Noah and those who were with him in the ark remained alive.

24 And the waters prevailed on the earth one hundred and fifty days.

7:10 *The waters of the flood were on the earth.* Some have suggested that the 'flood' (Heb. *mabbul*) was a scouring of the earth and that the waters then came after that. This verse does not support such a concept. The waters themselves are the *mabbul* which sweeps across the world and drowns all land creatures in its path: 'the flood came and took [lit. 'took up'] them all away' (Matt. 24:39).

7:11 *In the six hundredth year of Noah's life, in the second month, the seventeenth day of the month.* The exact days are now recorded in the Flood year. This strongly suggests that Noah himself was recording the events as in a diary.

7:11 *The fountains of the great deep were broken up, and the windows of heaven were opened.* The exact nature of what took place cannot be proved conclusively, but a number of geologists think that 'the great deep being broken up' is referring to underground reservoirs or superheated water which shot up into the atmosphere due to the splitting of the continental plates. There is evidence of meteorite cratering in the sedimentary layers which were laid down in the Flood. An asteroid estimated to be about 2.5 miles (4 km) wide, leaving a crater 56 miles (90 km) in diameter, is known to have hit South Australia in layers near the beginning of the Flood.[1] A series of such impacts may have been the cause of the break-up of the earth's crust and the movement of the tectonic plates, coupled with extreme (and simultaneous) volcanic activity. It is possible that the asteroids that still circle the sun today between Mars and Jupiter are the remains of a planet which exploded. It is significant that the Moon and other planets and moons in the solar system show evidence of bombardment.

7:12 *Rain … forty days and forty nights*. Worldwide rain for forty days and nights leading to all the globe being covered in water has to be more than water held in the atmosphere at that time. This is why most commentators who accept that this is real history do not think this was a collapse of a vapour canopy. Rather it is thought that this was the downpour of water that had first been ejected up into the atmosphere as superheated steam from the fountains of the great deep under the earth.[2]

7:13 *The very same day*. The phrase 'the very same' is from the Hebrew *etsem*, meaning 'bone', so the literal rendering is 'in the bone of that day'. It is used in 17:23 of Abraham and circumcision, and in Exodus 12:41 and Joshua 5:11 at the beginning and the end of the forty years in the wilderness. Notably, the word is used in a literal sense in Psalm 34:20—'Not one of them [bones] is broken'—and applied to Christ on the cross in John 19:36. This underlines the authority of God's Word and emphasizes the strength of what God has said: what God has said, will happen, and His righteousness is never broken. He means exactly what He says in the promises and warnings He has given.

7:16 *The LORD shut him in*. When Noah and his family and the animals were all in the ark, God shut the door. He secures the ark and keeps them from danger. It is a reminder of Matthew 25:10: 'the door was shut.'

7:18 *The waters prevailed and increased greatly on the earth*. The flood waters now rise up even after the forty days of rain. This is the second period of the Flood year, after the initial destruction of the first forty days. Now the water level rises across the globe.

7:19 *The waters prevailed exceedingly … all the high hills*. The waters now can never cover the earth, so this means that the mountains and high hills were much lower before the Flood. It is important to realize there would have been no mountains of the height of Everest and deep valleys in the oceans as in the Atlantic and Pacific today. We have to remember the important verse 2 Peter 3:6: 'the world *that then existed* perished, being flooded with water' (emphasis added).

7:20 *The waters prevailed fifteen cubits upward.* The maximum depth above the highest hills was about 22 feet, half the height of the ark and thus probably approximately the draft of the ship.

7:20 *The mountains were covered.* Herein lies a key issue which shows that the local flood hypothesis is wrong. If one postulates a local flood, one has then to propose that Mount Ararat, which is in the vicinity of the landing site, had a similar elevation before and after the Flood (as these theorists deny large mountain building in such an event). Mount Ararat is now 17,000 feet (5,180 metres), so this view is forced to countenance a flood of a depth of approximately 17,000 feet—which clearly can no longer be termed 'local'!

7:23 *He destroyed all living things.* As one would expect, the sedimentary rocks all over the globe carry abundant evidence of fossilization. Creatures buried quickly with no time to avoid the underwater landslides give a snapshot of their activity just before they died: fish with details of their scales clearly visible, an ichthyosaur in the process of giving birth! Ammonites all in one great mass graveyard now in Jurassic cliffs near Whitby, North Yorkshire—and there are many similar instances all over the globe. All speak volumes of sudden destruction, with no time for the creature to die slowly and become a meal for another.

7:23 *Only Noah and those who were with him in the ark remained alive.* God's purposes were achieved, just as God had said.

7:24 *The waters prevailed ... one hundred and fifty days.* This is the end of the second inundatory stage of the Flood before the subsiding of the flood waters takes place.

Notes

1 See **Andrew Snelling,** 'Did Meteors Trigger Noah's Flood?', *Answers* 7, no. 1 (2012): 68–71.

2 See **Steve Austin et al.,** 'Catastrophic Plate Tectonics: A Global Flood Model of Earth History', *ICC Proceedings 1994* (Pittsburgh, PA: Creation Research Society, 1994), pp. 609–621; and **Bodie Hodge,** 'The Collapse of the Canopy Model', 25 September 2009, Answers in Genesis, http://www.answersingenesis.org/home/area/tools/flood-waters.asp.

Chapter 8

1 Then God remembered Noah, and every living thing, and all the animals that were with him in the ark. And God made a wind to pass over the earth, and the waters subsided.

2 The fountains of the deep and the windows of heaven were also stopped, and the rain from heaven was restrained.

3 And the waters receded continually from the earth. At the end of the hundred and fifty days the waters decreased.

4 Then the ark rested in the seventh month, the seventeenth day of the month, on the mountains of Ararat.

5 And the waters decreased continually until the tenth month. In the tenth month, on the first day of the month, the tops of the mountains were seen.

6 So it came to pass, at the end of forty days, that Noah opened the window of the ark which he had made.

7 Then he sent out a raven, which kept going to and fro until the waters had dried up from the earth.

8 He also sent out from himself a dove, to see if the waters had receded from the face of the ground.

9 But the dove found no resting place for the sole of her foot, and she returned into the ark to him, for the waters were on the face of the whole earth. So he put out his hand and took her, and drew her into the ark to himself.

10 And he waited yet another seven days, and again he sent the dove out from the ark.

11 Then the dove came to him in the evening, and behold, a freshly plucked olive leaf was in her mouth; and Noah knew that the waters had receded from the earth.

12 So he waited yet another seven days and sent out the dove, which did not return again to him anymore.

13 And it came to pass in the six hundred and first year, in the first month, the first day of the month, that the waters were dried up from the earth; and Noah removed the covering of the ark and looked, and indeed the surface of the ground was dry.

14 And in the second month, on the

twenty-seventh day of the month, the earth was dried.

15 Then God spoke to Noah, saying,

16 'Go out of the ark, you and your wife, and your sons and your sons' wives with you.

17 Bring out with you every living thing of all flesh that is with you: birds and cattle and every creeping thing that creeps on the earth, so that they may abound on the earth, and be fruitful and multiply on the earth.'

18 So Noah went out, and his sons and his wife and his sons' wives with him.

19 Every animal, every creeping thing, every bird, and whatever creeps on the earth, according to their families, went out of the ark.

20 Then Noah built an altar to the LORD, and took of every clean animal and of every clean bird, and offered burnt offerings on the altar.

21 And the LORD smelled a soothing aroma. Then the LORD said in His heart, 'I will never again curse the ground for man's sake, although the imagination of man's heart is evil from his youth; nor will I again destroy every living thing as I have done.

22 While the earth remains, seedtime and harvest, cold and heat, winter and summer, and day and night shall not cease.'

8:1 *God remembered Noah.* God always had his eye on Noah throughout, but particularly through that Flood year as the ark carried that precious cargo. Just as God later remembered Abraham (19:29), God now remembers Noah.

8:1 *The waters subsided.* The view of conservative scholars is that this third stage of the Flood year is what led to the formation of the world surface as we know it. Psalm 104:6–9 describes the waters standing 'above the mountains'; then these waters (v. 8) go up 'over the mountains; they [go] down into the valleys, to the place which You founded for them'. Henry Morris suggests that 'the earth's crust collapsed into the previous subterranean reservoir chambers, forming the present ocean basins and causing further extrusions of magma around their peripheries through openings in their floors. The lighter sediments in the sea troughs were forced upward by isostatic readjustment to form mountain ranges and plateaus' (*Defender's Study Bible*).

8:3 *The waters receded continually from the earth.* The scouring effect of the water run-off is seen across all the continents today. Many regard the 1-mile deep Grand Canyon to have been formed by the powerful cutting action of fast-moving waters into previously laid-down sediments. What we see left today are the sliced vertical faces of towering cliffs, as waters, initially held back by a natural dam, broke through and thundered into what is now the Pacific.

8:4 *The ark rested … on the mountains of Ararat.* Notice the diary-like entry. A modern way of writing the date would be that the ark rested on the mountains of Ararat on 17/7/600 (the 17th day of the 7th month in the 600th year of Noah's life). There is no conclusive proof that the remnants of the ark are still extant. The 'mountains of Ararat' could be in a number of regions in the Turkey/Armenia area. It is important to recognize that the mountain now called Agri Dagh (Mt Ararat) is a volcano of relatively recent origin, so any claims in that area are unlikely to be correct. The ancient name for these mountains in the Turkey/Armenia area could refer to several other mountain ranges in neighbouring countries. Some have argued that a rock formation at the Durupinar site near the border with Iran on lower undulating hills and a moving mud-flow is the petrified remains of the ark. However, no clear signs of man-made structures are evident. Others have argued that 2 Kings 19:37 and Isaiah 37:38 show the biblical Armenia to have been close to Assyria in northern Iraq and that the ark landed in the Zagros Mountains, which would then fit with the migration to Shinar, which is generally accepted to be Babylon in southern Iraq.[1] It is wise not to be dogmatic on any of these proposals. The wood is likely to have been used for building, though we should be open to the possibility that some remains may still be found.

8:5 *The tops of the mountains.* The three months of waters abating until the tops of the mountains were seen (on 1/10/600—the 1st day of the 10th month of the 600th year of Noah's life) and the caution in waiting forty days before opening the window of the ark, coupled with the necessity to check for a dry location for disembarkation using the raven and the dove (vv. 7–8), are again consistent with the Flood not being local in extent.

8:7–9 *Then he sent out a raven … He also sent out from himself a dove … But the dove found no resting place for the sole of her foot, and she* *returned into the ark to him.* The dove returned to the ark because she, unlike the raven, would not eat carrion. Here lies a picture of the believer and the unbeliever. The dove is a clean animal and will not feed on death; likewise the believer should be separate from sin and death. The raven touches death regularly and typifies the unbeliever.

8:12 *The dove ... did not return again to him anymore.* Another week and the dove comes back with an olive leaf. Yet another week and the dove does not return at all, meaning there is land available and plants growing.

8:13 *Noah removed the covering of the ark.* Using Noah's years and months as before, here is the diary entry for the notable day when Noah and his family removed the top of the ark and saw the new world for the first time—1/1/601.

8:14 *The earth was dried.* It is 27/2/601—one year and ten days since the beginning of the Flood.

8:16 *Go out of the ark.* Noah awaits God's instructions to move from the ark. It was almost five months after seeing the tops of the mountains that Noah and his family finally left the ark. Noah is still careful to honour God after the major catastrophe is over.

8:20 *Noah built an altar ... offered burnt offerings.* Noah looked to the Lord very firmly in these momentous days at the beginning of the new world. He must have been extremely grateful that the Lord had spared them after the immense upheaval of the previous year. The feelings of thankfulness must have been similar to those felt by the occupants of the *Mayflower* when in November 1620 they arrived at Cape Cod in America. Noah offered one of *all* the clean animals and birds to the Lord as a burnt offering. This was a very extensive offering marking great thanks and praise to God for His grace to the eight who had been saved.

8:21 *I will never again curse the ground for man's sake.* Note that God refers to the Flood as a curse on the ground. The first curse on the ground was in Eden after the Fall (Gen. 3), and that Edenic curse is now followed by the Flood, which God states is a second curse on the ground. God brought the year-long Flood, but He will not do this again. This is another indicator that the Flood must have been global, as local floods have happened since.

8:22 *While the earth remains.* The world is now to be a far more forbidding place than previously, but, now that it has been purged and cleansed from the wickedness and vile behaviour of the previous inhabitants, the Lord promises the continuity of predictable annual seasons and the rhythm of a predictable day and night. We do well to remember that that ante-diluvian world perished due to the judgement of God, and that the world we are in now is not what it once was: 'But the heavens and the earth which are now preserved by the same word, are reserved for fire until the day of judgment' (2 Peter 3:7).

Note

1   See **Russell Humphreys,** *Journal of Creation* 25, no. 3 (2011): 6–8.

Chapter 9

1 So God blessed Noah and his sons, and said to them: 'Be fruitful and multiply, and fill the earth.

2 And the fear of you and the dread of you shall be on every beast of the earth, on every bird of the air, on all that move on the earth, and on all the fish of the sea. They are given into your hand.

3 Every moving thing that lives shall be food for you. I have given you all things, even as the green herbs.

4 But you shall not eat flesh with its life, that is, its blood.

5 Surely for your lifeblood I will demand a reckoning; from the hand of every beast I will require it, and from the hand of man. From the hand of every man's brother I will require the life of man.

6 Whoever sheds man's blood, by man his blood shall be shed; for in the image of God He made man.

7 And as for you, be fruitful and multiply; bring forth abundantly in the earth and multiply in it.'

8 Then God spoke to Noah and to his sons with him, saying:

9 'And as for Me, behold, I establish My covenant with you and with your descendants after you,

10 and with every living creature that is with you: the birds, the cattle, and every beast of the earth with you, of all that go out of the ark, every beast of the earth.

11 Thus I establish My covenant with you: Never again shall all flesh be cut off by the waters of the flood; never again shall there be a flood to destroy the earth.'

12 And God said: 'This is the sign of the covenant which I make between Me and you, and every living creature that is with you, for perpetual generations:

13 I set My rainbow in the cloud, and it shall be for the sign of the covenant between Me and the earth.

14 It shall be, when I bring a cloud over the earth, that the rainbow shall be seen in the cloud;

15 and I will remember My covenant which is between Me and you and every living creature of all flesh; the waters shall never again become a flood to destroy all flesh.

16 The rainbow shall be in the cloud, and I will look on it to remember the everlasting covenant between God and every living

creature of all flesh that is on the earth.'

17 And God said to Noah, 'This is the sign of the covenant which I have established between Me and all flesh that is on the earth.'

9:1 *Be fruitful and multiply, and fill the earth.* This is a similar command to the one the Lord gave in the beginning to Adam (1:28). It is of God that the world is full of people.

9:3 *Every moving thing that lives shall be food for you.* Whereas before, man was vegetarian (1:29), now he is allowed to eat animal meat. This is probably due to the fact that the harsher and more rigorous conditions of the post-Flood climate necessitated high-energy protein intake.

9:5 *For your lifeblood I will demand a reckoning.* This indicates how serious was the bloodshed before the Flood. Now strict rules are given concerning the sanctity of human life. The blood of man represents his life. Since he alone is made in the image of God, his blood is not to be shed, and if it is shed by man or beast, that man or beast is judicially to be slain. In the preceding verse we see that animal blood was not to be eaten, since animals were to be used for sacrifice and blood atonement.

9:6 *Whoever sheds man's blood, by man his blood shall be shed.* The law of capital punishment, to be administered by man, has never been revoked by God. Though each individual case may warrant clemency due to possible mitigating circumstances, the basic right of governments to exact capital punishment as the penalty for murder cannot and should not be abrogated, according to this verse. In the New Testament, after the passing away of the Levitical sacrifices, the Noahic commands are still in force: the eating of meat is allowed (1 Tim. 4:3–4), blood is not to be eaten (Acts 15:19–20) and governments have authority to bear the sword judicially (Acts 25:11; Rom. 13:4).

9:9 *I establish My covenant with you and with your descendants after you.* God made a covenant with Noah in 6:18, and this is now extended to Noah's descendants. The promise not to destroy the world again with a Flood (8:22) is repeated in 9:9, 11. The post-Flood cosmos will be kept in a regular and predictable cycle of seasons, and will end by fire (2 Peter 3:7).

9:13 *I set My rainbow in the cloud.* God now brings a sign of His covenant mercy to the new human population. The rainbow which God produces is new, so this confirms that there was no rain before the Flood (2:5) in the sense of the downpours that we now experience. Before the Flood, there were rivers and a mist coming up from the ground to irrigate the plants (2:6). Now the appearance of the rainbow indicates a major change in climatic conditions which would involve much harsher weather conditions, but God also uses it as a symbol of His steadfast keeping of His promise to sustain the earth for man. This point is pertinent in the alarm raised by some concerning world climate change. Though we are not at liberty to misuse resources, the rainbow promise still stands.

The institution of the rainbow promise is another strong indicator that the biblical Flood must have been global in extent, since there have been local floods of enormous proportions repeatedly over the centuries. In recent times there was the Indian Ocean tsunami on 26 December 2004 which killed of the order of 250,000 people. The Sendai earthquake and tsunami of 11 March 2011 and the Malawi floods of January and February 2015 caused the deaths of many thousands. If the biblical Flood of Noah's day was only partial, the rainbow promise has been proven to be untrue; it is only when we accept that the Flood of Noah was indeed worldwide that the promise makes sense. Christ implies that the Flood was global when comparing it to His return in Luke 17, and Peter, writing in 2 Peter 3, draws the same comparison.

---

18 Now the sons of Noah who went out of the ark were Shem, Ham, and Japheth. And Ham was the father of Canaan.

19 These three were the sons of Noah, and from these the whole earth was populated.

20 And Noah began to be a farmer, and he planted a vineyard.

21 Then he drank of the wine and was drunk, and became uncovered in his tent.

22 And Ham, the father of Canaan, saw the nakedness of his father, and told his two brothers outside.

23 But Shem and Japheth took a garment, laid it on both their shoulders, and went backward and covered the nakedness of their father. Their faces were turned

away, and they did not see their father's nakedness.

24 So Noah awoke from his wine, and knew what his younger son had done to him.

25 Then he said: 'Cursed be Canaan; a servant of servants he shall be to his brethren.'

26 And he said: 'Blessed be the LORD, the God of Shem, and may Canaan be his servant.

27 May God enlarge Japheth, and may he dwell in the tents of Shem; and may Canaan be his servant.'

28 And Noah lived after the flood three hundred and fifty years.

29 So all the days of Noah were nine hundred and fifty years; and he died.

9:19 *From these the whole earth was populated.* The whole of the human population in this new post-Flood world has come from the three sons of Noah and their wives. As mentioned above at 5:32 it is probable that the age order of the sons was Japheth (meaning 'Enlarged', 'Beautiful'), then Shem ('Name', 'Renown') and then Ham ('Warm', 'Hot')—but see note below on 9:24. Given that the names carry meanings in the Hebrew, there is some indication here that, prior to Babel, the language in use was Hebrew. Concerning the filling of the earth, this is entirely possible— indeed, population statistics strongly support the biblical position that the world population came out of Mesopotamia around 4,500 years ago. The gene pool of the six people (three sons and their wives) is entirely adequate to give enough genetic variational potential for the current world population, and there is enough time to have reached the current (as at 2013) world population of 7 billion. Using a conservative average growth rate of only 0.5% per annum (a rate well below the current growth rate of approx. 1%), one can readily calculate that this is consistent with a growth from eight people to 7 billion people in 4,500 years.

9:21 *Then he [Noah] drank of the wine and was drunk.* This sad event shows that even godly Noah fell. It does not mean that alcoholic drink is wrong as such, but it does clearly teach that drunkenness is a sin. It shows, firstly, that drunkenness makes one unaware of what is happening; and the New Testament instructs that we must not misuse our bodies: 'Do you not know that your body is the temple of the Holy Spirit who is in you ...?' (1 Cor. 6:9); also Proverbs 20:1: 'Wine is a mocker, strong drink is a brawler, and whoever is led astray by it is not wise.' Secondly, it also shows that drunkenness is often linked to nakedness (see note above on 3:7) and immorality. As this is the first mention of wine and alcoholic intoxication, we do well to take note that the Lord is warning us concerning its dangers. Thirdly, it shows that shame is often associated with alcoholic excess. In this case it brings the downfall of Ham and his son Canaan.

9:22 *Ham ... saw the nakedness of his father.* If it was merely an accidental seeing of his father's nakedness, an honourable son would have respectfully covered him, as his elder brothers did. But verse 22 goes on to state that he 'told his two brothers outside'—and the word translated 'told' is the Hebrew word *nagad*, which has the sense of 'declare', 'announce' or 'publish'. John Gill and Adam Clarke in their commentaries agree that Ham took delight in announcing the shame of their father to his brothers (Hab. 2:15 again connects alcoholic drink and nakedness). Japheth and Shem then carry out the honourable act of covering their father without seeing him.

9:24 *Noah ... knew what his younger son had done to him.* It would seem there was something more that Ham did (probably some immoral act of some kind) which is not stated here. A veil is drawn over what it was, but Noah saw prophetically what would happen to the three sons. A curse is brought upon Canaan the son of Ham, so some think that Canaan was involved in some way in the indecent action of Ham. Alternatively John Gill suggests it is possible that when it says 'younger son', this is actually referring to Canaan, as the youngest grandson through Ham (see 10:6), and that it was he who did something to Noah and told Ham of his father's drunkenness, which Ham then broadcast. This would then explain the curse coming specifically upon Canaan.

9:25 *Cursed be Canaan.* The cursing of Canaan, the father of the Canaanites, who later would be subdued and driven out by Joshua. He would be a servant of servants. Note that this is not all the Hamites, so not Ethiopia (Cush), Egypt (Mizraim) or Libya (Phut). Many today in Africa (where the descendants are primarily from Ham) wrongly think that Ham was cursed; but it was Canaan, and his servitude was doubly foretold by Noah: he would be servant to Shem (9:26) and to Japheth (9:27).

9:27 *May God enlarge Japheth*. This is not just geographical but a reference to the dominance in the world intellectually of Japheth. Many leaders, scientists and philosophers have come from Aryan stock (Roman/Greek/European). Shem would carry the blessing of the godly line and the emphasis of his nature would be spiritual. Ham would dominate in terms of the physical world: explorers, builders and traders. Henry Morris makes the comment, 'Noah recognized that Ham, Japheth and Shem were dominated, respectively, by physical, intellectual and spiritual considerations, and so could see prophetically that these attributes would likewise be emphasized in the nations descending from them' (*Defender's Study Bible*).

Chapter 10

1 Now this is the genealogy of the sons of Noah: Shem, Ham, and Japheth. And sons were born to them after the flood.

2 The sons of Japheth were Gomer, Magog, Madai, Javan, Tubal, Meshech, and Tiras.

3 The sons of Gomer were Ashkenaz, Riphath, and Togarmah.

4 The sons of Javan were Elishah, Tarshish, Kittim, and Dodanim.

5 From these the coastland peoples of the Gentiles were separated into their lands, everyone according to his language, according to their families, into their nations.

6 The sons of Ham were Cush, Mizraim, Put, and Canaan.

7 The sons of Cush were Seba, Havilah, Sabtah, Raamah, and Sabtechah; and the sons of Raamah were Sheba and Dedan.

8 Cush begot Nimrod; he began to be a mighty one on the earth.

9 He was a mighty hunter before the LORD; therefore it is said, 'Like Nimrod the mighty hunter before the LORD.'

10 And the beginning of his kingdom was Babel, Erech, Accad, and Calneh, in the land of Shinar.

11 From that land he went to Assyria and built Nineveh, Rehoboth Ir, Calah,

12 and Resen between Nineveh and Calah (that is the principal city).

13 Mizraim begot Ludim, Anamim, Lehabim, Naphtuhim,

14 Pathrusim, and Casluhim (from whom came the Philistines and Caphtorim).

15 Canaan begot Sidon his firstborn, and Heth;

16 the Jebusite, the Amorite, and the Girgashite;

17 the Hivite, the Arkite, and the Sinite;

18 the Arvadite, the Zemarite, and the Hamathite. Afterward the families of the Canaanites were dispersed.

19 And the border of the Canaanites was from Sidon as you go toward Gerar, as far as Gaza; then as you go toward Sodom, Gomorrah, Admah, and Zeboiim, as far as Lasha.

20 These were the sons of Ham, according to their families, according to their languages, in their lands and in their nations.

21 And children were born also to Shem, the father of all the children

of Eber, the brother of Japheth the elder.

22 The sons of Shem were Elam, Asshur, Arphaxad, Lud, and Aram.

23 The sons of Aram were Uz, Hul, Gether, and Mash.

24 Arphaxad begot Salah, and Salah begot Eber.

25 To Eber were born two sons: the name of one was Peleg, for in his days the earth was divided; and his brother's name was Joktan.

26 Joktan begot Almodad, Sheleph, Hazarmaveth, Jerah,

27 Hadoram, Uzal, Diklah,

28 Obal, Abimael, Sheba,

29 Ophir, Havilah, and Jobab. All these were the sons of Joktan.

30 And their dwelling place was from Mesha as you go toward Sephar, the mountain of the east.

31 These were the sons of Shem, according to their families, according to their languages, in their lands, according to their nations.

32 These were the families of the sons of Noah, according to their generations, in their nations; and from these the nations were divided on the earth after the flood.

10:1 *This is the genealogy of the sons of Noah.* A further *toledoth* closing off the period of the Flood and moving on to the origin of the nations from the three sons of Noah. The commentary that follows has drawn much from information contained in the writings of Henry Morris—his commentary (*Defender's Study Bible*) and his books *The Bible and Modern Science* (Moody, 1951) and *Science and the Bible* (Moody, 1986).[1]

10:2 *The sons of Japheth.* Gomer is the ancestor of the Celts; his name is linked to the Welsh word for the Welsh language, Cymraeg, a corruption of 'Gomeraeg'. The Greek historian Herodotus identified Gomer with Cimmeria, a name linked to the Crimea and also to Galatia (part of Turkey), where in Roman times some of the Gauls lived; and to Gaul (France) and Galicia (North-West Spain).

10:2 *Magog.* He lived in the North (Ezek. 38:15). Josephus links Magog with Scythia, which is Romania and the Ukraine.

10:2 *Madai.* The ancestor of the Medes, which is one part of the Medo-Persian kingdom (Dan. 6:8, 12, 15). The Medes later settled parts of India, which even today has a mixture of Median and Dravidian people (see note below at 10:7).

10:2 *Javan* is the Hebrew name for Greece (so in Dan. 8:21, the 'king[dom] of Greece' is literally the 'king[dom] of Javan').

10:2 *Tubal* is probably connected to Iberia (Georgia). Josephus has their name as Thobelites. The capital of this area today is Tbilisi, which is clearly connected to the name 'Tubal'. Later migration led to them crossing the Caucasian mountains over the river still called 'Tobol' today, to the city of Tobolsk in Siberia.

10:2 *Meshech* is probably connected to Moscow and the Meschera lowland.

10:2 *Tiras* is linked to Thrace in the country of Macedonia today.

10:3 *Ashkenaz* is the Hebrew for the area which is now Germany.

10:3 *Riphath* is associated by Josephus with Paphlagonia, which is an area in what is now northern Turkey running along the southern coast of the Black Sea.

10:3 *Togarmah*. The Armenians have a strong tradition that they are descended from Togarmah, the third son of Gomer.

10:4 *Elishah* is linked to one of the Greek peoples named in Homer's *Iliad*, 'the Eilesians'.

10:4 *Tarshish* is immediately identified with the area around Tarsus in the region of Cilicia (in modern-day Turkey).

10:4 *Kittim* is the biblical name for Cyprus.

10:5 *The coastland peoples of the Gentiles* primarily refers to the sons of Japheth and the European dispersion, but later the term 'Gentiles' refers to all non-Israelites.

10:6 *Ham*. The Scriptures often refer to Africa as the land of Ham (Ps. 105:23, 27; 106:22).

10:6 *Cush* is the eldest son of Ham and is the biblical name for Ethiopia.

10:6 *Mizraim* is the second son of Ham. Mizraim is the biblical name for Egypt (50:11).

10:6 *Put*. Josephus records that Put is the old name for Libya, and the ancient river Put was in Libya. By Daniel's day, the name had been changed to Libya (Dan. 11:43).

10:6 *Canaan* settled in what is today Israel and Jordan. They were later conquered by Joshua as judgement for their evil practices and immorality.

10:7 *Sons of Cush.* These five descendants of Cush (Seba, Havilah, Sabtah, Raamah and Sabtechah) settled initially in Arabia, with Seba later migrating to Sudan—hence the name Sabeans in Isaiah 45:14. Cush is the biblical name for Ethiopia, so there was some migration to other parts of East Africa. There is also evidence that descendants of Ham migrated to India and formed the Dravidian culture. One of the mountain ranges in Central Asia is called the Hindu Kush; and the ancient Sanskrit texts *Ramayana* and *Mahabahrata* refer to the Rama Empire in ancient India, which is thus connected to the migration of Raamah.

10:7 *Sheba and Dedan.* In Abraham's day, two of his grandsons were named after these sons of Cush (25:3).

10:8 *Nimrod … began to be a mighty one.* The actual name Nimrod is associated by rabbinical commentators with 'rebellion' or 'let us rebel'.[2] His name is preserved in many legends from Babylonia and he was undoubtedly the first great emperor after the Flood. Legends state that after his death he was deified and worshipped as Merodach or Marduk.[3] His name is possibly also linked to Osiris, the god of the underworld in Egyptian idolatry, and some think that the Hindu god of destruction, Shiva, is also the deified Nimrod.

10:9 *A mighty hunter before the* LORD. Nimrod is not only associated with feats of great physical valour in hunting, but he does this 'before the LORD'—literally 'in the face of the LORD'. He is an evil man fighting against God, as Josephus recounts (*Antiquities* 1.4.2). Some argue he is in fact the vile person Gilgamesh in the Babylonian *Epic of Gilgamesh* who is determined to fight against Huwawa, who is recounted in that epic as bringing the Flood.[4] Others suggest Nimrod was Sargon the Great, the first king of Sumer and Akkad, c.2300 BC.[5] One cannot be dogmatic as to Nimrod's identity, but it is clear that Nimrod was the first mighty king after the Flood, a violent hunter who set himself up against God, and that he led the building of the tower of Babel.

10:10 *The beginning of his kingdom was Babel.* The might of Nimrod is seen in the building of Babel, which was his capital city, and the tower of Babel in the land of Shinar (11:1–4) in the Tigris–Euphrates valley. Shinar is a term for Mesopotamia's southern plain and is equivalent to

Sumer. This early Sumerian culture was then the first main kingdom after the Flood, and it is significant that the final fall of all world systems against God is pictured by the fall of Babylon in Revelation 18, the city that typified the start of rebellious idol worship by Nimrod at the beginning.

10:10 *Erech, Accad, and Calneh*. Erech is 'Uruk', which is 100 miles south-east of Babylon and the location of the Gilgamesh writings. Accad is linked to the Akkadian Empire, which is probably the same as the Sumerian kingdom. It is not known where Calneh was.

10:11 *Assyria [Asshur, KJV] … Nineveh*. Asshur was a son of Shem (10:22) so this verse seems to indicate that Asshur had settled in Nineveh in an area 200 miles north of Babylon, but Nimrod went into Asshur and invaded it, annexing it to his own kingdom. This would later become Assyria. The city Nineveh is named after Nimrod's son Ninus.

10:12 *Calah*. Though Rehoboth and Resen have not been identified, Calah has been excavated and is called Nimrud, located on the river Tigris in what is now northern Iraq.

10:13–18 *Mizraim*. Here are listed the descendants of Mizraim. Most of them are difficult to trace in secular records since they migrated deeper into Africa. It is known that the Pathrusim dwelt in Pathros, which is Upper Egypt, and the Caphtorim are identified with the Philistim (Philistines) in the Bible. Secular historians identify the Philistines with Crete, so these people evidently migrated from Egypt to Crete and then to the eastern shore of the Mediterranean.

10:15 *Sidon*. Firstborn of Canaan. Sidon still exists today and was the chief city of the Phoenicians.

10:15 *Heth* is the ancestor of the Hittites, who were a great empire in Asia Minor for over eight hundred years. When that empire crumbled, many went east. They are identified in Egyptian inscriptions as 'Kheta' and in Babylonian as 'Khittae', which is probably linked to 'Cathay', the old name for China. Secular archaeologists note similarities between the Mongols and the Hittites.

10:15–18 *Sidon his firstborn … the Jebusite, the Amorite, and the Girgashite … Sinite*. Eleven sons of Canaan are listed in verses 15–18 and were conquered later by Joshua. The Amorites are referred to in secular records as the Amurru. The Sinites may have been connected to the wilderness of Sin and possibly Mount Sinai, and there was an Assyrian god called 'Sin'. The Sinites could be connected with the reference to Sinim (Isa. 49:12), which is another name for China.

10:21 *Shem, the father of all the children of Eber.* Eber is the origin of the name 'Hebrews'.

10:22 *Elam, Asshur, Arphaxad, Lud, and Aram.* Elam is part of Persia (now Iran); Asshur became Assyria, but his settlement was taken over by Nimrod (see 10:11); Arphaxad is linked to the Chaldeans; Lud is the origin of Lydia in what is now western Turkey; and Aram is the old name for Syria. The Aramaic language is named after Aram and was used very widely across the Ancient world (2 Kings 18:26; and Christ speaking on the cross in Mark 15:34).

10:23 *Uz.* This is the name for Job's homeland (Job 1:1).

10:25 *Peleg.* This name means division and probably means that the division of Babel took place in his time.

10:25 *In his days the earth was divided.* The word 'divided' is *palag* in the Hebrew and also has the sense of 'to split up'; many think that after the Babel division of languages there was a journeying far and wide across the globe to chart out new territory.

10:29 *Sons of Joktan.* The thirteen sons of Joktan are believed to have settled in Arabia, and possibly their offspring are not listed because Shem, the head of that family, was close by.

10:32 *According to their generations, in their nations.* This chapter has given the true origin of the nations of the world. Not all details are there but there is sufficient structure for all to see what our true origins are as a human race after the Flood.

Notes

1 See also **Harold Hunt and Russell Grigg,** 'The Sixteen Grandsons of Noah', *Creation* 20, no. 4 (1998): 22–25; also available at http://creation.com/the-sixteen-grandsons-of-noah.

2 See **Gesenius,** *Hebrew and Chaldee Lexicon.*

3 **Morris,** *Defender's Study Bible,* and **Alexander Hislop,** *The Two Babylons* (1871).

4 See **David Livingston,** 'Who Was Nimrod?' in *Bible and Spade,* Summer 2001; and available online at Associates for Biblical Research, https://www.biblearchaeology.org/post/2006/10/30/who-was-nimrod.aspx#Article.

5 **Douglas Petrovich,** *Journal of the Evangelical Theological Society* 56, no. 2 (2013): 273–305.

Chapter 11

1 Now the whole earth had one language and one speech.

2 And it came to pass, as they journeyed from the east, that they found a plain in the land of Shinar, and they dwelt there.

3 Then they said to one another, 'Come, let us make bricks and bake them thoroughly.' They had brick for stone, and they had asphalt for mortar.

4 And they said, 'Come, let us build ourselves a city, and a tower whose top is in the heavens; let us make a name for ourselves, lest we be scattered abroad over the face of the whole earth.'

5 But the LORD came down to see the city and the tower which the sons of men had built.

6 And the LORD said, 'Indeed the people are one and they all have one language, and this is what they begin to do; now nothing that they propose to do will be withheld from them.

7 Come, let Us go down and there confuse their language, that they may not understand one another's speech.'

8 So the LORD scattered them abroad from there over the face of all the earth, and they ceased building the city.

9 Therefore its name is called Babel, because there the LORD confused the language of all the earth; and from there the LORD scattered them abroad over the face of all the earth.

11:1 *One language and one speech.* All the people had one language (Heb. *saphah*, 'lip') and one speech (Heb. *dabar*, 'word'). The double statement gives great force and emphasis to what Nimrod had done in establishing a one-world dictatorship under himself. Many think that the language could have been Hebrew since the names of many people and locations have great descriptive depth in that language.

11:2 *Plain in the land of Shinar.* This is generally accepted to be in southern Iraq, in the valley where the Tigris and Euphrates flow.

11:3 *Let us make bricks.* God's altars were never made of brick

(Exod. 20:25) but were always of natural stone. God's later house (the temple) was made of shaped stone, but even then the working of the stone was not done at the temple site ('built with stone finished at the quarry', 1 Kings 6:7).

11:4 *Let us build ourselves a city, and a tower … let us make a name for ourselves.* The emphasis of this verse is 'us'. It is man making a name for himself; it is not for the glory of God but is man-centred worship. The building of Babel (10:10), and in particular the tower of Babel, was undoubtedly a religiously inspired act of Nimrod. The words 'whose top is in the heavens' indicate that it would have been of some height. However, the emphasis is not so much on the height but on what the 'top' of the tower (Heb. *rosh*, 'head', 'chief') was for. It was to study the heavens, almost certainly for the study of the stars and astrology. Most think it was for the accurate watching of the stars to try to predict whether warning of another catastrophe similar to the recent Flood could be gained. Discovered ancient towers and ziggurats often have emblems of creatures marked on them which many think are to do with the signs of the zodiac and were distorted into worship of the stars.

11:4 *Lest we be scattered abroad over the face of the whole earth.* This is outright rebellion in the light of God's explicit command in 9:1.

11:6 *One language.* The unity of the rebellion is the main reason for judgement—hence the Lord breaks their communication lines in the next verses. Unity of purpose is invariably aided greatly by a common language.

11:6 *Now nothing that they propose to do will be withheld from them.* The warning here is similar to what the Lord said of man before the Flood (6:5). These verses underline that man's heart is profoundly wicked and naturally in rebellion against God. The scattering of the people is to diminish the concentration of evil which the tower represented. It is always the intention of the devil to attempt the overthrow of God's rule on earth, and towards the end he will again seek to establish world domination by the Antichrist (2 Thes. 2:4; Rev. 13:3, 8).

11:7 *Confuse their language.* This is a miraculous act of God and implies that the basic language units are not connected. Some have suggested that the seventy names listed in Genesis 10 represent the languages that the Lord created in Genesis 11. There was sufficient distinctive vocabulary and phonology (the sound of the words) that they could not carry on building. The study of languages points to their origin in the Middle East.[1]

11:8 *The LORD scattered them abroad.* They are now forced to do what God had originally intended. No doubt Nimrod remained with his immediate tribe, and probably the Sumerian civilization is the remnant of his empire. Still today in Iraq, there is a mound at Borsippa, seven miles south of Babylon, called 'Birs-nimrud'. The excavation of this and other ancient Babylonian ziggurats shows that Nimrod's Sumerian Empire is associated with the ruins of Babylon today. Herodotus (440 BC) described a tower still visible 300 feet high that was reckoned then to be the remains of the tower of Babel built by Nimrod around 2200 BC.

11:9 *Its name is called Babel.* Some sceptics have tried to make out that Babel means 'gate of God'. Instead it is another example of an onomatopoeic word (like *nacham* in 6:6) where the sound of the word itself suggests what it means—in this case the transliteration into English carries the same sound as 'babble'. The word *babel* is used in Hebrew to mean 'mixed' or 'confusion'.

11:9 *The LORD scattered them abroad over the face of all the earth.* No doubt this took some centuries to achieve, but records show that the ancients were far more masterful in travel both on land (maybe making use of land bridges due to lower sea levels in the one Ice Age following the Flood) and by sea than has generally been acknowledged. It is known that the Phoenicians and Egyptians built sea-going ships and that ancient exploration led to the making of archaeological sites such as the megalithic constructions on Easter Island in the Pacific, at Stonehenge in England and at Göbekli Tepe ('Potbelly Hill') in Turkey; as well as the ancient city of Tiahuanaco at 12,500 feet (3,810 metres) in Bolivia (which includes African-looking faces carved into the rocks, indicating an early Hamite civilization), the dry stone walls using massive irregular size blocks at Sacsayhuamán in Peru, the city Machu Picchu 7,970 feet (2,430 metres) high up in the Andes in Peru, the Giza pyramids of Egypt, with enormous carefully carved blocks fitted together inside them, and the Mayan astronomical observatory at Chichen Itza in Mexico, whose accuracy is as good as that of modern observatories.[2] These sites indicate that very advanced technology existed right from the beginning.

Henry Morris makes an important summary of these times: 'All carried essentially the same Babylonian culture and pagan religion with them, unfortunately, so that Babylon is called in the New Testament (Rev. 17:5) "the mother of harlots and abominations [i.e. idolatries] of the earth". At the same time they carried a faint remembrance of the true God and His promises, especially remembering the divine judgment of the great Flood in their traditions' (*Defender's Study Bible*).

---

10 This is the genealogy of Shem: Shem was one hundred years old, and begot Arphaxad two years after the flood.

11 After he begot Arphaxad, Shem lived five hundred years, and begot sons and daughters.

12 Arphaxad lived thirty-five years, and begot Salah.

13 After he begot Salah, Arphaxad lived four hundred and three years, and begot sons and daughters.

14 Salah lived thirty years, and begot Eber.

15 After he begot Eber, Salah lived four hundred and three years, and begot sons and daughters.

16 Eber lived thirty-four years, and begot Peleg.

17 After he begot Peleg, Eber lived four hundred and thirty years, and begot sons and daughters.

18 Peleg lived thirty years, and begot Reu.

19 After he begot Reu, Peleg lived two hundred and nine years, and begot sons and daughters.

20 Reu lived thirty-two years, and begot Serug.

21 After he begot Serug, Reu lived two hundred and seven years, and begot sons and daughters.

22 Serug lived thirty years, and begot Nahor.

23 After he begot Nahor, Serug lived two hundred years, and begot sons and daughters.

24 Nahor lived twenty-nine years, and begot Terah.

25 After he begot Terah, Nahor lived one hundred and nineteen years, and begot sons and daughters.

26 Now Terah lived seventy years, and begot Abram, Nahor, and Haran.

27 This is the genealogy of Terah: Terah begot Abram, Nahor, and Haran. Haran begot Lot.

28 And Haran died before his

father Terah in his native land, in Ur of the Chaldeans.

29 Then Abram and Nahor took wives: the name of Abram's wife was Sarai, and the name of Nahor's wife, Milcah, the daughter of Haran the father of Milcah and the father of Iscah.

30 But Sarai was barren; she had no child.

31 And Terah took his son Abram and his grandson Lot, the son of Haran, and his daughter-in-law Sarai, his son Abram's wife, and they went out with them from Ur of the Chaldeans to go to the land of Canaan; and they came to Haran and dwelt there.

32 So the days of Terah were two hundred and five years, and Terah died in Haran.

11:10 *The genealogy of Shem.* The *toledoth* marking the end of the section describing the time of the Babel dispersion and the beginning of the genealogy of Shem's line.

11:10 *Shem was one hundred years old.* See the discussion of the age order of the sons of Noah in the notes above on 5:32 and using the fact from 7:6 that Noah was 600 years old when the Flood came. Shem was probably the middle son.

11:13 *After he begot Salah, Arphaxad lived four hundred and three years.* The years each patriarch lived now reduces steadily after the Flood. This was probably due to the large climatic changes from the even temperatures before the Flood to the harsher climate afterwards. The soils were probably very rich in nutrients before the Flood; also, mutations were now increasing in the inbreeding population.

11:14 *Salah.* This genealogy is similar in construction to that in Genesis 5. From Jude 14 we saw that there were no gaps from Adam to Enoch and, by implication, since the style is similar, we can assume that there are no gaps in the rest of Genesis 5 and Genesis 11. The names are repeated in 1 Chronicles 1 and Luke 3 (Mary's blood line), further indicating that there are no gaps. There is one difference: Luke 3:36 has an extra name, 'Cainan', between Arphaxad and Shelah (Salah). It is likely to be a copying error since it is not found in either Genesis 11:14 or 10:24; neither does 1 Chronicles 1:18 have Cainan inserted, and nor do any of the Masoretic manuscripts. Most of the Septuagint (Greek versions of the OT) manuscripts do insert the name in Genesis 11, but interestingly the earliest Septuagint manuscripts do not, which suggests that the Masoretic manuscripts are correct and that a mistake was made in the copying of the original Greek translation which filtered through into Luke 3:36. There is an in-depth article on this matter by Larry Pierce[3] and Jonathan Sarfati has also written a good summary.[4]

11:16 *Peleg*. Most think that 10:25 means the Babel dispersion took place in Peleg's time. It is noteworthy that there is a big drop in lifespan at this period from the father of the Hebrews, Eber (464 years), to Peleg (239 years). This may well be because of the changes in living conditions after the dispersion, and possibly the greater difficulty in living for the people now scattered and separated across the Middle East and beyond. As noted at 9:19 above, the present world population (as at 2013) of 7 billion and estimated world population plots working backwards for the last few thousand years are entirely consistent with man having emerged out of the Mesopotamian plains between four and five thousand years ago— but not at all consistent with the idea of man having emerged 200,000 years ago, as evolutionists would have us believe.

11:26 *Terah lived seventy years, and begot Abram, Nahor, and Haran*. Though Abram is listed first we do not know the age order of these children.

11:27 *This is the genealogy of Terah*. Another *toledoth* marking the end of the list of patriarchs from Shem to Abram and the beginning of the descendants of Abram.

11:28 *Haran died before his father Terah*. Haran died in Ur of the Chaldeans. The land of Haran is mentioned later, in 11:31. Therefore it is likely that Haran had migrated westwards, but had come back to visit Terah in Ur, where he then died. His son Lot then became attached to Abram.

11:29 *Abram and Nahor took wives*. Abram married his half-sister (20:12) and Nahor married his niece (Milcah, the daughter of Haran). These are close marriages but not yet genetically dangerous enough for prohibition. Such prohibitions came later (Lev. 18:6–16) since by that time genetic mutations had sufficiently increased to cause significant malformations in birth from such close relatives intermarrying.

11:31 *And Terah took Abram his son ... and they went forth with* *them from Ur of the Chaldees*. Not much is known about Terah. It can be inferred that Terah also received an initial call of God to go to Canaan, as the text expressly states that the intent was to go there. They came to the land of Haran and dwelt there. Had Terah lost heart? Had the resolve not been maintained? There is a clear suggestion this was the case since the Lord expressly tells Abram to leave Haran in 12:1–4, after Terah has died (Acts 7:4). Careful comparison of Genesis 11:26, Genesis 12:4 and Acts 7:4 (see also Gen. 25:7) shows that Abram is seventy-five years old when he leaves Haran and that this is not long after the year of Terah's death (2,083 years after creation). This then means that Abram must have been born when Terah was 130 years old, which, though unusual by this period in the patriarchs, is possible (we note later that Isaac is born when Abram is 100, Gen. 21:5). When Abram leaves Ur of the Chaldeans we note that Eber is still alive, which therefore shows that the idolatrous worship had infected most of the original godly seed of Shem.

11:32 *Terah died in Haran*. Of this series of ten generations—Noah to Abram—remarkably the early generations (Shem to Eber) are still living as Terah initially departs from Ur of the Chaldeans (11:31–32). Noting the comment above at 5:29, we see the plausible communication of the early records of the events of the pre-Flood and immediately post-Flood world to Abram involving as few as four people: Adam speaking with Methuselah, Methuselah with Shem, and Shem with Abram. That Moses then compiled these documents and passed them carefully down the generations means that we should take them very seriously indeed. Christ said, 'But if you do not believe his [Moses'] writings, how will you believe My words?' (John 5:47).

A note on the historical timelines of Genesis 5 and 11

The genealogies of Genesis 5 and 11 show that there were roughly a thousand years from the creation of Adam to Noah's birth, and then approximately a further thousand years from the birth of Noah to Abram's birth. Exodus 12:40 and Galatians 3:17 combined with 1 Kings 6:1 indicate that, though we may struggle with the exact chronology of the time of the judges, there were roughly another thousand years from the time of Abram to the time of David, with Solomon following him with the building of the first temple. The time of David was approximately one thousand years before Christ. This means that, though Archbishop Ussher may have been pressing the text too much concerning the exact day of creation, he was right in overall terms: today we are at a time of the order of six thousand years since creation.[5]

Notes

1 See, for instance, **Thomas Gamkrelidze and V. V. Ivanov,** 'The Early History of Indo-European Languages', *Scientific American,* March 1990, p. 10; and **Donald Chittick,** *The Puzzle of Ancient Man* (3rd edn; Newberg, OR: Creation Compass, 2006), p. 152.

2 Details of these and other important sites which date back to the third millennium BC can be explored in books such as **Chittick,** *The Puzzle of Ancient Man,* and **Barry Fell,** *America BC: Ancient Settlers in the New World* (New York and London: Pocket Books, 1989).

3 **L Pierce,** 'Cainan in Luke 3:36: Insight from Josephus', in *Journal of Creation* 13, no. 2 (1999): 75–76.

4 **Dr Jonathan Sarfati,** 'Cainan: How Do You Explain the Difference between Luke 3:36 and Gen. 11:12?', Creation.Com, http://creation.com/cainan-can-you-explain-the-difference-between-luke-336-and-genesis-1112, accessed October 2015.

5 More details can be found on this in *Genesis for Today.*

Closing remarks

Genesis is foundational to all Christian doctrine. The origin of the entire universe, including the plant and animal kingdom, the importance of man, the role of man, his relationship to his Creator as well as to the world and animals: all is portrayed here in Genesis. The origins of sin and death are also clearly revealed; and no other book has this coherent record of the early development of man before and after the worldwide Flood, with the promise and revelation unfolding of redemption through the blood sacrifice of the Lamb of God promised in Genesis 3:15.

Though revival is always God's prerogative, Brian Edwards showed in his book *Revival: A People Saturated with God*[1] that revival has only ever taken place when the Lord's people have believed in the totality of Scripture. In our day and age, Genesis is one of the main books in the firing line, as atheists and humanists dismiss it as irrelevant. What is a deep tragedy in the twenty-first-century West is that evangelical Christians have also relegated Genesis and no longer look upon it as the book of beginnings. Christ referred to the writings of Moses in a very serious way at the end of the account He told of the rich man and Lazarus in Luke 16:31: 'If they do not hear Moses and the prophets, neither will they be persuaded though one rise from the dead.' If we do not believe Moses, we are in a serious condition of unbelief, and God will not bless us with the revival that is so essential in our churches today. As believers we need individually and corporately to repent and turn back to this ancient book of beginnings.

Note

1 Darlington: Evangelical Press, 2000.